EARLY CHILDHOOD E

MW00667120

SHARON RYAN, EDITOR

Pre-K Stories: Playing with Authorship and Integrating Curriculum in Early Childhood
DANA FRANTZ BENTLEY & MARIANA SOUTO-MANNING

Ready or Not: Early Care and Education's Leadership Choices—12 Years Later, 2nd Ed.
STACIE G. GOFFIN & VALORA WASHINGTON

Teaching STEM in the Preschool Classroom: Exploring Big Ideas with 3- to 5-Year-Olds
ALISSA A. LANGE, KIMBERLY BRENNEMAN, & HAGIT MANO

High-Quality Early Learning for a Changing World: What Educators Need to Know and Do
BEVERLY FALK

Guiding Principles for the New Early Childhood Professional: Building on Strength and Competence
VALORA WASHINGTON & BRENDA GADSON

Leading for Change in Early Care and Education: Cultivating Leadership from Within
ANNE L. DOUGLASS

When Pre-K Comes to School: Policy, Partnerships, and the Early Childhood Education Workforce
BETHANY WILINSKI

Young Investigators: The Project Approach in the Early Years, 3rd Ed.
JUDY HARRIS HELM & LILIAN G. KATZ

Continuity in Children's Worlds: Choices and Consequences for Early Childhood Settings
MELISSA M. JOZWIAK, BETSY J. CAHILL, & RACHEL THEILHEIMER

The Early Intervention Guidebook for Families and Professionals: Partnering for Success, 2nd Ed.
BONNIE KEILTY

STEM Learning with Young Children: Inquiry Teaching with Ramps and Pathways
SHELLY COUNSELL ET AL.

Courageous Leadership in Early Childhood Education: Taking a Stand for Social Justice
SUSI LONG, MARIANA SOUTO-MANNING, & VIVIAN MARIA VASQUEZ, EDS.

Teaching Kindergarten: Learner-Centered Classrooms for the 21st Century
JULIE DIAMOND, BETSY GROB, & FRETTA REITZES, EDS.

Healthy Learners: A Whole Child Approach to Reducing Disparities in Early Education
ROBERT CROSNOE, CLAUDE BONAZZO, & NINA WU

The New Early Childhood Professional: A Step-by-Step Guide to Overcoming Goliath
VALORA WASHINGTON, BRENDA GADSON, & KATHRYN L. AMEL

Eight Essential Techniques for Teaching with Intention: What Makes Reggio and Other Inspired Approaches Effective
ANN LEWIN-BENHAM

Teaching and Learning in a Diverse World, 4th Ed.
PATRICIA G. RAMSEY

In the Spirit of the Studio: Learning from the *Atelier* of Reggio Emilia, 2nd Ed.
LELLA GANDINI ET AL., EDS.

Leading Anti-Bias Early Childhood Programs: A Guide for Change
LOUISE DERMAN-SPARKS, DEBBIE LEEKEENAN, & JOHN NIMMO

Exploring Mathematics Through Play in the Early Childhood Classroom
AMY NOELLE PARKS

Becoming Young Thinkers: Deep Project Work in the Classroom
JUDY HARRIS HELM

The Early Years Matter: Education, Care, and the Well-Being of Children, Birth to 8
MARILOU HYSON & HEATHER BIGGAR TOMLINSON

Thinking Critically About Environments for Young Children: Bridging Theory and Practice
LISA P. KUH, ED.

Standing Up for Something Every Day: Ethics and Justice in Early Childhood Classrooms
BEATRICE S. FENNIMORE

FirstSchool: Transforming PreK–3rd Grade for African American, Latino, and Low-Income Children
SHARON RITCHIE & LAURA GUTMANN, EDS.

The States of Child Care: Building a Better System
SARA GABLE

Early Childhood Education for a New Era: Leading for Our Profession
STACIE G. GOFFIN

To look for other titles in this series, visit www.tcpress.com

continued

Everyday Artists: Inquiry and Creativity in the Early Childhood Classroom
DANA FRANTZ BENTLEY

Multicultural Teaching in the Early Childhood Classroom
MARIANA SOUTO-MANNING

Inclusion in the Early Childhood Classroom
SUSAN L. RECCHIA & YOON-JOO LEE

Language Building Blocks
ANITA PANDEY

Understanding the Language Development and Early Education of Hispanic Children
EUGENE E. GARCÍA & ERMINDA H. GARCÍA

Moral Classrooms, Moral Children, 2nd Ed.
RHETA DEVRIES & BETTY ZAN

Defending Childhood
BEVERLY FALK, ED.

Don't Leave the Story in the Book
MARY HYNES-BERRY

Starting with Their Strengths
DEBORAH C. LICKEY & DENISE J. POWERS

The Play's the Thing
ELIZABETH JONES & GRETCHEN REYNOLDS

Twelve Best Practices for Early Childhood Education
ANN LEWIN-BENHAM

Big Science for Growing Minds
JACQUELINE GRENNON BROOKS

What If All the Kids Are White? 2nd Ed.
LOUISE DERMAN-SPARKS & PATRICIA G. RAMSEY

Seen and Heard
ELLEN LYNN HALL & JENNIFER KOFKIN RUDKIN

Supporting Boys' Learning
BARBARA SPRUNG, MERLE FROSCHL, & NANCY GROPPER

Young English Language Learners
EUGENE E. GARCÍA & ELLEN C. FREDE, EDS.

Connecting Emergent Curriculum and Standards in the Early Childhood Classroom
SYDNEY L. SCHWARTZ & SHERRY M. COPELAND

Infants and Toddlers at Work
ANN LEWIN-BENHAM

The View from the Little Chair in the Corner
CINDY RZASA BESS

Culture and Child Development in Early Childhood Programs
CAROLLEE HOWES

Educating and Caring for Very Young Children, 2nd Ed.
DORIS BERGEN, REBECCA REID, & LOUIS TORELLI

Beginning School
RICHARD M. CLIFFORD & GISELE M. CRAWFORD, EDS.

Emergent Curriculum in the Primary Classroom
CAROL ANNE WIEN, ED.

Enthusiastic and Engaged Learners
MARILOU HYSON

Powerful Children
ANN LEWIN-BENHAM

The Early Care and Education Teaching Workforce at the Fulcrum
SHARON LYNN KAGAN, KRISTIE KAUERZ, & KATE TARRANT

Windows on Learning, 2nd Ed.
JUDY HARRIS HELM, SALLEE BENEKE, & KATHY STEINHEIMER

Supervision in Early Childhood Education, 3rd Ed.
JOSEPH J. CARUSO WITH M. TEMPLE FAWCETT

Guiding Children's Behavior
EILEEN S. FLICKER & JANET ANDRON HOFFMAN

The War Play Dilemma, 2nd Ed.
DIANE E. LEVIN & NANCY CARLSSON-PAIGE

Possible Schools
ANN LEWIN-BENHAM

Everyday Goodbyes
NANCY BALABAN

Playing to Get Smart
ELIZABETH JONES & RENATTA M. COOPER

The Emotional Development of Young Children, 2nd Ed.
MARILOU HYSON

Young Children Continue to Reinvent Arithmetic—2nd Grade, 2nd Ed.
CONSTANCE KAMII

Bringing Learning to Life
LOUISE BOYD CADWELL

The Colors of Learning
ROSEMARY ALTHOUSE, MARGARET H. JOHNSON, & SHARON T. MITCHELL

A Matter of Trust
CAROLLEE HOWES & SHARON RITCHIE

Embracing Identities in Early Childhood Education
SUSAN GRIESHABER & GAILE S. CANNELLA, EDS.

Bambini: The Italian Approach to Infant/Toddler Care
LELLA GANDINI & CAROLYN POPE EDWARDS, EDS.

Serious Players in the Primary Classroom, 2nd Ed.
SELMA WASSERMANN

Young Children Reinvent Arithmetic, 2nd Ed.
CONSTANCE KAMII

Bringing Reggio Emilia Home
LOUISE BOYD CADWELL

Pre-K Stories

Playing with Authorship and Integrating Curriculum in Early Childhood

Dana Frantz Bentley
Mariana Souto-Manning

Teachers College Press
Teachers College | Columbia University
New York and London

Published by Teachers College Press, 1234 Amsterdam Avenue, New York, NY 10027

Cover design by Rebecca Lown. Watercolor lettering by Lana Smirnova and photo of children by Rawpixel, both via Shutterstock.

All photos by Lucinda Burk.

Chapter 1 contains a figure adapted from "Toward Praxically-Just Transformations: Interrupting Racism in Teacher Education," by M. Souto-Manning, 2018, *Journal of Education for Teaching*, *45*(1), 97–113. Reprinted with permission of Taylor & Francis Ltd, http://www.tandfonline.com.

Library of Congress Cataloging-in-Publication Data

Names: Bentley, Dana Frantz, author. | Souto-Manning, Mariana, author.
Title: Pre-K stories : playing with authorship and integrating curriculum in early childhood / Dana Bentley, Mariana Souto-Manning.
Description: New York : Teachers College Press 2019. | Series: Early childhood education series
Identifiers: LCCN 2019017190 (print) | LCCN 2019980882 (ebook) | ISBN 9780807761311 (paperback) | ISBN 9780807761328 (hardcover) | ISBN 9780807777718 (ebook)
Subjects: LCSH: Early childhood education--Curricula. | Language arts (Early childhood)
Classification: LCC LB1139.4 .B46 2019 (print) | LCC LB1139.4 (ebook) | DDC 372.21--dc23
LC record available at https://lccn.loc.gov/2019017190
LC ebook record available at https://lccn.loc.gov/2019980882

ISBN 978-0-8077-6131-1 (paper)
ISBN 978-0-8077-6132-8 (hardcover)
ISBN 978-0-8077-7771-8 (ebook)

Printed on acid-free paper
Manufactured in the United States of America

We dedicate this book to the children
whose ideas, stories, play, and authorship teach us
both on these pages and in the world beyond them.

Contents

Acknowledgments

As illustrated in the pages of this book, our writing is about stories—the many stories that fill the lives of young children and of the teachers who have the opportunity to teach and learn with them. So are our appreciations here, filled with the many stories of the people, small and grown-up, who made this book possible—across time and space.

We begin by thanking the children and families who are represented on these pages and the many children and families who shape us as educators, writers, and thinkers. It is a privilege to work with young children, to be shaped by their perspectives, and to be coauthors with them, storying the world in our collaborations. We will continue to learn from their authorship, battling sharks in dramatic play and finding the perfect block elevations for stage building in the Cozy Corner. We thank them for sharing their worlds with us and for allowing us to be the kind of adults who always get to play. We are honored to be authors *with* them.

We also thank the incredible editors at Teachers College Press who supported us throughout this process. We are grateful for Susan Liddicoat's thoughtful, precise editing and the way it allowed our work to evolve. With a book such as this, it is so easy to become too close to the text. Her perspective helped us step back to make the work more accessible, and we are so grateful. Emily Spangler's kindness and patience with us have been without bounds. We thank Emily for allowing us to be mothers, teachers, and professors, as well as authors, as we slowly made our way through this process. We so appreciate her understanding and how it allowed us to finally complete this book.

In what follows, we take a step back from the "we" of this book to offer our individual acknowledgments.

Dana: I do not have enough words to thank my coteacher, Lucinda Burk, who was my support and collaborator in bringing this work to life in the pre-K classroom. Not enough is said about coteachers and the incredible relationship that springs up when we teach together every day. Lucinda, thank you for your wisdom, your gentleness, and your ability to help us all slow down and listen more carefully to the children. Thank you for the constant silent messages, conveyed with just a look, that are a part of coteacher talk.

Thank you for tearing up with me at our students' impromptu achievements and for our relationship, which continues to make me a better teacher and person. I am always grateful for you.

I want to thank my family, Nick, Davey, and Ellie, for all that you are and all that you help me to be. Of all my roles in the world, being a part of our family is the most important and most rewarding. Our everydays together are the best of days. Thank you for being my team.

While I still have the floor, I need to acknowledge and thank the incredible Mariana Souto-Manning, whom I am privileged to call my mentor and coauthor. Once upon a time, many years ago, Mariana agreed to allow me to sit in on a graduate course that I could not afford to even pay for. Sometimes you meet someone and you just know, "I need to be in your presence," and so it was when I met Mariana. Those early moments irrevocably changed my thinking and the trajectory of my work as an educator. Mariana, thank you for helping me to find my voice, and for validating that voice as I work in the murky space of the teacher-scholar. Our collaborations are some of the most meaningful in my life. I hope to continue to work with you and to learn from you for many years to come. Thank you for being in my life.

Mariana: I thank my children, Lucas and Thomas Souto Manning, for inspiring me to be fully present with young children as they navigate and author the world—for showing me their brilliance and competence as sophisticated meaning-makers and knowledgeable symbol-weavers. You have inspired me to ask questions, to look closely, to listen carefully, and to commit to learning humbly from and with young children, their families, and communities. Although you are no longer young children, you continue to teach me how to be a better person each and every day. I also thank you for how you have shared your excitement for my work and allowed me the time to document and write stories (such as the ones contained in this book). Thank you for understanding that more than anything, I want to share my learnings with others in hopes of transforming education in ways that fully honor the brilliance of young children. Thank you for loving, supporting, and dreaming with me. I also thank your dad, whose support over the years allowed all of us to grow.

I acknowledge the influence of my professional family—the teachers with whom I've had the privilege of learning, building, and growing across time and space. I continue to be indebted to their questions and inspired by their drive. Dana Frantz Bentley is one of the teachers with whom I had—and continue to have—the privilege of learning and growing. I acknowledge her influence and thank her for being an inspiring teacher and a wonderful friend. I still remember the day when Dana approached me about sitting in on my class. And I am so glad she did. Teacher learning (beyond initial teacher preparation) is so important, yet not as available as it should be. In my career, I have tried to cultivate and sustain learning communities of teachers committed to bettering the lives and futures of minoritized communities; although these communities helped support the development of practicing teachers, in truth, they have also sustained me. In these communities I have had the opportunity to engage humbly, with the understanding that "no one knows it all; no one is ignorant of everything" (Freire, 1998, p. 39). In such communities, I was able to engage as teacher-learner and as learner-teacher, blurring traditional boundaries. Dana and I were part of such a community. Although the "class" she joined concluded well over 10 years ago, we continue to collaborate and grow beyond the bounds of any formal timeline, because research and learning are grounded in relationships and relationships last beyond the so-called "schedule" of projects. In humanizing research, there is no "exit strategy"; relationships do not end when projects are set to. And so it is with Dana and I. Our relationship is authentic; our questions are critical and urgent. I am privileged to call Dana my friend, coauthor, and cothinker. From the day we met and the semester we shared to our long phone calls, meetings, and many coauthored pieces over the course of 2 decades, I am truly thankful for her influence in my life . . . and look forward to future opportunities for learning and growing with her.

Introduction

For over 30 years, educators have known that "the gradual process of becoming a communicator begins at birth" (Genishi & Dyson, 1984, p. 2). By the time young children enter preschool, they are already skilled storytellers and story-actors. They ask questions as ways of securing audiences ("Guess what?!" and "You know what?"). They make bids for coauthorship ("I'll be the momma and you be the daughter"). They actively recruit audiences ("Come see the carnivores; they are trying to escape!"). They author their own identities ("I am an archeologist digging for fossils with a chisel") as they take on roles that require the resignification of materials in their world (the sand table becomes a site where dinosaur fossils can be dug out, and the blocks become a fortress for "very bad tigers"). They develop as authors within social and cultural contexts, interactionally. They braid social symbols to develop complex storylines that contain sophisticated pragmatic, semantic, and syntactic understandings. That is, their storylines display knowledge of how languages are used within and across social contexts (pragmatics), they understand the aspect of grammar that pertains to how words and sentences communicate meaning (semantics), and they know how to organize elements of language (such as words) to form sentences that can be understood and are deemed to be appropriate within and across languages (syntax).

Yet, we adults seldom recognize their brilliance or appreciate their language repertoires and communicative practices. We often think of what they need to know—to succeed in kindergarten, to become successful students in school. In doing so, we take a readiness approach, seeking to arm children with (often decontextualized) practices and skills that will help them in kindergarten (Graue, 1992). That is, we ignore how education (especially in preschool and pre-K) is not preparation for life, but life itself, as John Dewey (1938) wrote almost a century ago.

In the race to achieve at faster and faster rates, we seem to have forgotten the importance of identifying and honoring children's communicative strengths, of cultivating and sustaining their unique and culturally situated ways with words (Heath, 1983). We seem to have forgotten that teachers should attend to "the rhythms and rhymes of their developing students" (Genishi & Dyson, 2012, p. 20). Yet, in early childhood classrooms, each and every day, "teachers and children adapt to each other, even as they sometimes move to a rhythm all their own. The teacher responds, leads, and sometimes lets go to observe more carefully the rhythms of children in motion . . . spread[ing] their skilled, responsive movement across times and spaces" (p. 20).

As young children enter preschool and pre-K, too often they are regarded as empty vessels within which knowledge is to be deposited and developed. They are assessed for what they do not have, instead of what they do have. Rejecting this view, which Freire (1970) described as the banking approach to education, we (Dana and Mariana, the authors) call for preschool and pre-K teaching to recognize children's prior experiences, practices, and communicative repertoires, building on them and cultivating them.

"At a time of life when we credit them with little intelligence, children master a most complex and sophisticated system of sounds and meanings" (Genishi & Dyson, 1984, p. 1). They author stories through play. They are, as Dyson (1990a) proposed, symbol-readers and symbol-weavers. They weave drawings, notes, and symbols as they seek to communicate. They author long before they recognize the written symbolic system. In fact, not all of their symbols are written down, and some of these symbols are not even recognized by adults as symbols.

In this book, we unveil the ways in which young children work together to collaboratively conceive and develop stories years before they make their way into the bound pages of a book. We invite you, the reader, to slow down and attend to the rhythms and timelines young children negotiate as they develop as authors. Rejecting the simplistic and reductionist equating of reading and writing letters and words as comprising authoring, we theorize from classroom practices and offer a more expansive and child-centered definition of *authoring*. We do so not as a way of replacing adult definitions of authoring (which tend to equate writing with authoring). Instead, we seek to honor children's ways with words, their conceptualizations, and their development of stories as ways of making sense in and of the world.

We invite you to enter Pre-K East, Dana's classroom in Cambridge, Massachusetts. In doing so, we seek to shed light onto the ways in which young children are knowledgeable authors and capable curriculum coconstructors. Although this practice has been proposed with older children—for example, Emdin (2016) proposed cogenerative lessons in high school science—Dana and her teaching partner, Lucinda Burk, engage in cogenerating curriculum *with* young children.

As we explore examples and stories from the Pre-K East classroom, we address theories of early communication and spoken and written language in preschool and pre-K. Theorizing from examples, we offer an overview of how very young monolingual and multilingual learners communicate and develop their language practices and repertoires. Through these classroom experiences, we examine how young children navigate within and across communicative repertoires. We showcase practices and curricula that promote communication, talk, and emergent literacy in educational settings for children with a range of abilities. We delve into the powerful everydayness of language and communication, mining the richness of daily classroom life for the foundations of integrated curricula. As we do so, we engage a sociocultural framework for teaching in the multiple contexts in which children learn and in which adults and children can work toward social justice.

STORYING THE PRE-K EAST CLASSROOM

Pre-K East is situated in an independent school. In this classroom, stories are centered and young children are positioned as capable authors. Instead of employing adult-centered and sanctioned definitions of authoring, which often regard authoring as a synonym for writing, in the Pre-K East classroom, children's voices and actions are regarded as authoring. The focus of this book is on Dana's practices and her interactions with the children of Pre-K East. In the following narrative and the other narratives that shape this book, Dana writes in first person, reflecting on the conception of stories within the context of pre-K.

Heroic Sharks and Superheroes: The Story Is Conceived

It was 11:00 A.M. in the pre-K classroom, and the space had taken on what I think of as the mid-morning hum of activity. After exploring different options, testing materials for classroom play, and shifting alliances, the children had settled into the groove of focused play. The air felt thick with ideas and intentions. Mindful of the children's focus, I picked my way around the room, sometimes chatting, offering new materials, or asking a question, but mostly just listening to the children at work. As I peered into "Big Blocks," our large hollow-block play area, the light shone down on a huddle of small heads, deep in conversation.

"Let's play that you're the bad shark, okay?" announced Simon,[1] the benevolent leader of the group.

"But I don't want to be the shark. I like to be good guys," was Frank's tentative yet firm response.

"Okay, but there needs to be a bad guy. So, let's play that you're the bad shark but he gets good again," Simon reasoned.

"Yeah! And then he's friends with the superheroes, but the other bad guys don't know he's really a good guy!" crowed Frank, pleased with the reframing of his character.

---

1. All children's names are pseudonyms.

Not to be left out, Rachel stood a bit taller and offered, "Yeah, and let's play that we're the family, and I'm the big sister who can be the babysitter."

This plotline shift silenced the discussion, several of the boys who were playing appearing unconvinced.

"But we're playing that it's a boat. With a bad shark and superheroes. We're not playing family," explained Simon patiently.

"Yes, but the superheroes have to rescue somebody. And I'm the babysitter and this is the baby for getting rescued."

This retort solved the problem, and the huddle continued, the voices even more animated than before.

"Okay, then, there's the superheroes, the bad shark who gets good, the babysitter, and the baby for getting rescued. So let's play that. . . ."

A Place of Story

The early childhood classroom is a place of story (Paley, 2004). Stories quite literally construct the days in the Pre-K East classroom, from bad sharks secretly helping superheroes to babysitters being rescued on boats in shark-infested waters. Characters are conceived, heroes and villains stalk the classrooms, plots are developed and executed, and the bodies of stories come to life at the hands and minds of young children. This is the life of the early childhood classroom. It is a sophisticated practice of independent and collaborative storytelling and story writing at which young children are adept (Paley, 1990; Souto-Manning, 2013).

As an early childhood teacher for over 17 years, Dana is party to these secrets, to the richness and complexity of the stories that populate the life of pre-K. As a teacher, she began to ask questions about how these stories could come to life in the context of young children's work in language arts. After all, these are the stories that matter to them, the stories they deem significant. Through their practice, Dana and her coteacher Lucinda asked:

- How could this active practice of play and storytelling be seen as language and literacy work?
- How could these young storytellers come to understand themselves as readers and authors through their play?
- How might children's stories be centered in integrated curricula?

These were the questions that guided their work.

As the teachers began to ask these questions about storytelling, they were struck by the simplicity of the solution to locating language arts in the authentic life of the early childhood classroom. Language arts live in children's play. The elements of a story—the characters, setting, plotline, problem, resolution—all of these elements and more live in children's play, often in highly sophisticated ways. The high level of motivation and criticality with which young children approach their play (Dewey, 1902) is exactly the kind of focus that teachers seek in the deep learning of academic concepts and skills within and across content areas. The children, deep in the thick of developing play characters, solving problems, and developing a plot, literally propel themselves into the zone of proximal development (Vygotsky, 1978). It is up to teachers to harness this thinking, to purposefully connect it to the language arts curriculum, and more important, to children's understandings of themselves as readers and authors.

Who Are We?

In these pages, you will find many "wes." There is the "we" of the children, the "we" of the classroom community, the "we" of the teachers, and the "we" of the teacher and teacher educator, the researchers who coauthored this text. The Pre-K East classroom is taught by a team of coteachers (Dana and Lucinda), both of whom participated in the shaping of the practices present in this text. However, Dana is also a coauthor of this book, and so her voice can be heard throughout the text, both in the narratives from the Pre-K East classroom as well as in the reflections and theoretical discussions of the classroom practice. Dana is joined by Mariana, who coauthored this book; Mariana weaves in a broader theoretical perspective on the early childhood theory and practice. Through these collaborations, through these "wes," the authors weave layered representations of the work of educators, and the possibilities alive in young children's play, in Pre-K East and beyond.

Languaging, Literacies, and Play

In this book, we (the authors, Dana and Mariana) look at language arts and literacy through the lens of play. We look at how children *language*—how they make meaning and make sense in and through play. In doing so, we join a long tradition of (re)positioning children's play at the center of the early literacy curriculum (Cooper, Capo, Mathes, & Gray, 2007; Dyson, 1990b; Genishi & Dyson, 2009; Marsh, 2005; Paley, 2004, 2014; Souto-Manning & Yoon, 2018; Wohlwend, 2013). But we do so at a unique time—at a time in which there have been unprecedented investments in preschool and pre-K.

Although we both agree with the importance of investments in early childhood education, we also see such investments coupled with greater pressure to academize the early childhood classroom. After all, these investments are often justified by cost-benefit analyses, which show that every dollar of investment made in early years' education corresponds to a savings of many more dollars later on. Longitudinal studies have shown that graduates of early childhood programs such as the Perry Preschool Program and the Abecedarian Project experienced gains in intelligence and achievement, had lower school retention rates, were less likely to be identified with a disability, and had higher rates of high school graduation (e.g., Barnett, 1996; Campbell, Breitmayer, & Ramey, 1986; Campbell & Ramey, 1994, 1995; Clarke & Campbell, 1998). Though this commodification of early childhood education has led to increased funding and programming, it has also amounted to—from our perspectives—restrictive notions of what counts as teaching, what is regarded as evidence of learning, and what is seen as literacy.

It is within this context that in this book we seek to

- defend child-centered early childhood education,
- explain how children's meaning-making processes correspond to adult notions of literacy (instead of simply imposing adult notions of language arts and literacy onto children), and
- offer insights into the expansive capacity of young children.

Even within this child-centered context, Dana must address the realities of outside pressures and expectations around skill acquisition and kindergarten "readiness." As she focuses on children's play and meaning-making, Dana is always concerned about her students' development of skills, their needs as learners, and the expectations they will face as they move through their schooling experience. Simply put, the pressure is real.

When Dana considers language arts and literacy in her classroom, she works with her students to devise rich, relevant experiences with language and literacy (broadly conceived); these experiences inspire young children to see writing and language as serving communicative purposes (Halliday, 1993), as tools for their own thinking and expression (Vygotsky, 1978). It is from this perspective that we invite you to journey with us into Dana's Pre-K East classroom.

THE JOURNEY

This book follows the story of one pre-K classroom as Dana, Lucinda, and their students (ages 4 and 5) coconstructed a language and literacy curriculum through children's stories, analysis of literature, and perspectives on the purpose of authoring as a whole. Using the children's stories as a foundation, the teachers and children built their own literacy curriculum, exploring not simply stories, but the reasons for writing, for books, and for publishing. This encompassing perspective on literacy brought about a naturally integrated approach to curriculum, an approach that makes visible the ways that stories, languages, and words live and work across seemingly discrete academic spaces. As they worked together, they questioned curricular norms. In doing so, the children were invited to challenge existing rationales for developing as literate beings (for example, "So that you can have a publishing party in 1st grade") and develop new, child-centered reasons for their work as authors and readers.

As academic standards and restrictive notions of literacy push their way more deeply into the early childhood classroom, it becomes essential to find ways in which the authenticity of children's play and expression can serve as the foundation for academic concepts (Bodrova, 2008; Diamond, 2010; Hatch, 2002; Souto-Manning, Lugo Llerena, Martel, Salas Maguire, & Arce-Boardman, 2018; Souto-Manning & Martell, 2016; Souto-Manning & Yoon, 2018). When children are given autonomy through critical, authentic work around academic concepts and constructs, they are empowered to shape a curriculum that might otherwise dominate them. Through this process, young children come to understand themselves as thinkers with the ability to act upon curriculum in order to critically construct knowledge (Souto-Manning, 2010).

Through critical conversations, Dana, Lucinda, and the children collaborated in connecting the vitality of the children's oral language and storytelling to elements of print, writing, and publishing (Genishi & Dyson, 2009; Lindfors, 2008). As the children connected their play and storytelling identities to print and writing, traditional "literacy work" took on an urgency that shaped the children's relationship to language arts (Dyson, 1994b). Through reflective, critical pedagogy, culture circles were coconstructed to address the genuine purposes of literacy in the lives of young children (Freire, 1970; Souto-Manning, 2010). Concepts of authorship and literacies wound their way naturally across classroom work, creating an organic pathway to curriculum integration. The story of this classroom illustrates the ways literacy can take on meaning within the context of children's storytelling and play, which afford critical perspectives on literacy and language arts (Genishi & Dyson, 2009; Lindfors, 2008).

A Roadmap

The purpose of this book is to help readers envision ways they may engage in the process of coconstructing such a curriculum with their students. Although we do not believe in how-tos or step-by-step (often overly simplistic) directions for engaging in this work, we hope that the rich examples from Pre-K East will shed light on the power, the possibility, and the necessity of centering young children and play in the early literacy curriculum. Specifically, our book follows the process of The Book Project, a child-centered, semester-long integrated project. As you will see, it particularly dominated the work of the Pre-K East classroom during the second semester of the school year.

In Part I, we begin by explaining the process by which a child-centered project was born, as well as the critical thinking that the children did around the purposes of literacy and language arts. Because we want to make clear that the coconstructed, emergent curriculum is highly intentional, and based upon specific classroom practices that frame and inspire this kind of work with young children, in Part I we offer foundational practices that situate teachers, children, and a classroom community as ready to engage in this kind of coconstructed curricular work together.

Part II moves into the content of The Book Project itself; through classroom narratives and the children's publications, we explore the daily experiences of generating this project with the children. As you will see, each book illustrates an integrated approach to language arts and literacy work in the early childhood classroom, responding to the interests and pursuits of the children, as well as the academic needs of, and pressures imposed on, the class. As the literacy work in the classroom developed through play and stories, the children began to author an integrated approach to their own learning.

In Part III we offer broader reflections on the practices and intentions around this kind of work with young children. We consider Dana's perspective as the teacher as well as the social impact of the work and the shape of children's acquisition of skills. With the children, we look back on their work, and outward to the broader implications of these practices in early childhood.

Our Intentions

As you explore these pages, it will become visible that as the pre-K children worked, their ideas served as the stimulus for academic connections and challenges. In cogenerating curriculum with children, Dana and Lucinda deliberately and purposefully centered their questions, voices, and interests. Taking a "yes, and" approach, the teachers invited the children to do more, to engage in thinking more deeply and critically. Through coconstructed classroom practices, the children knew that their teachers offered these invitations to further the children's work and the children's goals for themselves. Each teacher question or challenge was directly linked to the goals the children had developed themselves within the work of the project.

The story of the Pre-K East classroom is offered as a window—a way of seeing how the process of fostering authorship in a pre-K classroom while centering children's voices, interests, and questions might evolve—rather than as a direct instruction of how to teach. The nature of this practice is situational; the story will be different in every classroom, responding to the storytelling of the children and teachers in that environment. This is the beauty of this language arts and literacy curriculum: It belongs wholly to the individual classroom. The book is punctuated by the stories of this particular classroom, not to require repetition, but in order to spark imagination.

We invite you to read for possibility, looking not for what should be done, but for what might be possible. As you read, we hope you will see yourself, your classroom, and the children in your class reflected in these moments, inspiring unique directions and interpretations that meet the needs of your practice.

But before we move ahead, let's return to the heroic sharks and superheroes conceived by the children of Pre-K East. The sharks are alive and well, their story still winding its way through the children's play. After all, it is only by learning from the children that we can fully understand how the story begins.

The Sharks Return

It was 12:15 P.M., and we absolutely had to clean up. The children were so engaged that I hated to stop them, but if we didn't clean up now, we'd never have time for outdoor play, lunch, and rest. I reluctantly rang the bell, and turned on the music to remind the small bodies of the intended purpose of this time. As the mass chaos began, there were cries from Big Blocks.

"Dana! Dana, can you come quick?!?"

I hurried to Big Blocks and found Simon and Rachel standing, arms spread wide to protect their structure from the overzealous cleaning of their classmates. Knocking down block structures is one of the few appealing elements of clean-up time.

"Take a picture!" Rachel cried, swatting away a would-be cleaner. "We aren't done with this structure. We're not done with the story!"

"Yeah," added Simon, looking menacingly at possible destructors. "The baby just got captured and we didn't rescue her yet. We can't just leave her there! Can you take a picture of our structure so we can make it again tomorrow?"

"Then we can rescue the baby," Rachel added, making sure that I understood.

"Of course," I replied, snapping a series of photos with my phone. Unconvinced, Simon took the phone and scrolled through the pictures.

"You missed the crib and the shark catcher," he told me. "Can I take a few more pictures?"

I nodded, and as I did, Simon physically moved me into his spot, stretching my arms out to protect the structure. Then he took the requisite shots, checking his work as he went.

"Okay, that's it," he announced, signaling the beginning of the demolition.

I moved out of the way as boat, crib, and shark catcher came crashing down. When clean-up was finally finished, Rachel sat down next to me with a sigh.

"Whew!" she said. "I'm glad we got those pictures of the structure. We want to finish our game. We're definitely not done with it."

"I wonder," I asked, "do you think you'd like to write your story down? You could tell me the words, and then I could either write them on the computer or on paper. Then you would have the words to your story, and the pictures."

"Well," said Rachel, considering—inviting grown-ups into play is always a situation requiring careful thought. "I need to ask Simon, 'cause he's really the boss of the game. But that might be good. Then we could play our game on playdates and stuff, not just at school. Then we would know how the game goes."

And thus, the story begins. . . .

Part I

"How Do Stories Come into Our Class?"

Laying the Foundations

The three chapters in Part I focus on the classroom environment, community, and practices that enable the kind of curriculum that supports young children's development as authors. We look closely at the practical elements of communication, interaction, and classroom organization that support teachers in creating a play-based, child-centered language arts curriculum. Chapter 1 addresses three building blocks critical to the kind of literacy work we propose in pre-K classrooms: emergent curriculum, culture circles, and project work. It explains how these come together and function to foster a pre-K classroom that supports young children as authors.

Chapter 2 examines the unique shape of authorship within this text and within the Pre-K East classroom. In this chapter, we explore the act of storying in play, addressing the meaning and foundations of play-based authorship. We look closely at the role of the teacher as sponsoring and sanctioning this particular definition of authorship. We also identify particular classroom practices that make the role of stories visible in the daily lives of the Pre-K East children.

Chapter 3 provides windows into how, as a class, Dana and her students collectively interrogate the purpose of books, publishing, language, stories, and writing. Through critical conversations, the classroom community explores and develops a shared understanding of the purpose of authoring, empowering them to challenge schemas or symbols of books and allowing children to create meaning and understanding collaboratively. This serves as a starting point for their work.

CHAPTER 1

The Classroom and Its Practices

The work of building literacy curricula out of the play of young children is born of particular ways of thinking about children, of understanding their work, of learning about their interests and abilities, of mapping the shape of their community, and of negotiating power in the classroom. That is, it is predicated on seeing children as capable and positioning them agentively (as human beings who can do things). It requires humbly recognizing that "no one knows it all; no one is ignorant of everything" (Freire, 1998, p. 39), thus requiring learning from and with young children while deliberately rejecting assumptions and stereotypes of young children as incapable or unready. It can only happen if we understand the community in which we teach, and within the context of such a community, problematize traditional power structures and assumptions that children bring with them to the early childhood classroom about how classrooms work, who holds the power, and who has the answers. It entails fundamentally transforming what we do.

To bring these abstract concepts to life within the context of Pre-K East, we begin this chapter with a story from Dana's classroom. This story happened in September, 3 days after the start of the school year and long before The Book Project took off. Yet we offer it here because it provides a window into a tiny moment that began to shape the children's thinking about their play, responsibilities, and power in this classroom community. It was foundational to the work of The Book Project.

"We Can Be in Charge Because This Is the Kids' Work": The Great Sand and Water Catastrophe

It was a hot September day and the kids were sitting in a circle on the purple rug, flushed and expectant. No matter how powerful the air conditioning, the heat of 16 small bodies, all invigorated by play, has the effect of turning the classroom into a sauna. The heat only added to the agitation in the room.

There was a problem. There was a steady drip, drip, drip from the sink heard over the kids' heated breathing, followed by a dribble, dribble of water and sand making its way across the linoleum floor. They looked up at me, all flushed cheeks and expectant eyes, almost calm in the order of things.

"Somebody's in trouble!" their eyes said with confidence. And this was the moment: the moment when things began to change, the moment when I had the opportunity to invite them to consider shifting their perspective of who they are in the classroom, of who they are as learners.

"So," I began carefully, "it seems like you're worried about something. What do you feel worried about?"

A hand immediately shot into the air. "She did it!" shouted Susan, crisp in her lavender bows and accusations, although not yet confident in names on this first week of school. "That girl," she pointed, awaiting the effect.

I smiled and said, "Oh, I'm not worried about that. It seems like some people were just trying things out. No big deal. Do you guys want to explain your ideas?"

There was a moment of silence. A moment of, "Wait, isn't somebody getting in trouble?" and then a cascade of excited explanation, sometimes—but not always—accompanied by hand-raising. We were still working on that, but give us a break. It was the third day of school.

"See, there was sand in the sand table, but we wanted a volcano . . ."

"Yeah, yeah, but you need wet sand for a volcano because the dry stuff just falls down . . ."

"And we sawed the sink over there . . ."

"That's kind of far from the sand table, so we just taked the sand over there to get it wet . . ."

"Oh, oh, and then we was gonna take it back to the sand table and we did, but it didn't all get into the table . . ."

"Yeah, some of it got stucked in the sink, and then the water got bigger, and BIGGER!"

With the possibility of "trouble" off the table, the process, theories, and effects of the kids' work had the chance to grow, and the class listened and discussed avidly, awaiting the inevitable conclusion.

"And then WHOOOSH, there was a waterfall!" Peter's voice reached a crescendo. "And now there's so much sand and water on the floor," he finished quietly, the concept of "trouble" once again rearing its head after his dramatic finish.

They all looked again at me, ready again for the inevitable scolding. "It had to be coming, right?" their eyes said. With concern and confidence, they waited for me, their teacher, to establish the power structure.

"So, what do you guys think? What do you want to do?" I asked.

There was quiet again at the question, and Susan's hand shot again into the air. "That was bad. They need time out," she explained to me firmly, trying so hard to keep her teacher on track. Clearly, I did not know how these things work.

"Hmmm," I said. "Well, were they trying to do something wrong?" I asked. Heads shook: no.

"We was just trying to make sand wet!"

"Yeah, like an experiment."

"So," I continued, "did the experiment work?"

"Yeah!" said Francis. "The sand is so, so wet now. But there's a big mess and we can't use the sink because it's gross! So, we better clean that up so we can use it later." This statement was supported by the group, nodding their agreement.

"But do you want to have wet sand to use?" I asked. "Because that seems like a good idea. How could we still do your idea tomorrow?"

"Hey, maybe there could be some water in the sand table, too!" Claire suggested.

"Yes, in a bowl so it's not a mess," Susan added, with tentative enthusiasm. This was still all highly abnormal.

"Okay, so tomorrow, I should put the sand in the sand table, with a bowl of water, too?" I checked.

"Okay!" shouted Peter. "Now let's clean up the mess! We can be in charge because this is the kids' work!"

The class rushed forward in chaos, water slopping and wet sand crunching. It was not a simple, or particularly effective, clean-up that day, but it was done together, by those who made the mess, and those who did not. And if the mess was bigger at the end of "clean-up" than it was at the beginning, perhaps that was not the point. Sometimes coming together, thinking together, and making together is more important than the outward performance of cleanliness and organization.

SMALL MOMENTS AND EVERYDAY STORIES LEAD TO BIG CURRICULA

This is a story Dana loves to tell because it is a story that so nearly did not happen. This story-that-almost-wasn't was fundamental to the identity of the classroom community that ultimately undertook The Book Project. It was emblematic of how the classroom community came to work through its own iteration of Freirean culture circles (Freire, 1970; Souto-Manning, 2010). In this story, the children in Pre-K East engaged in reading their worlds, doing all of the following:

- Undertaking a thematic investigation (What was important and urgent within the context of that specific community?)
- Identifying a generative theme (What was most important and most urgent for that particular classroom community at that very moment?)
- Problematizing the situation (Why *and* how had that happened?)
- Dialoguing (Whose voices have we considered and whose perspectives and stories are missing?)

- Problem solving together (What can *we* do to address this problem?)
- Negotiating a plan for action (What do *we* want to do to address the situation?)

This process is illustrated by Figure 1.1.

This is a story that could have been stopped, that Dana almost stopped so many times in her desire to take on the traditional "teacher" role. Those traditional impulses were absolutely there. She reflects:

> I nearly leapt in when I saw the children carrying the sand to the sink. I sighed inwardly as water and sand were tracked across the classroom floor. I then watched with dread as the sink filled, and water poured onto the classroom floor. I also wanted to kindly sit before the class and make a rule: "No sand in the sink."

Then, she offered, "I wanted to do all of these things, but I held back because a story was being made. It was a story about experimentation, about problem solving, about collaboration, and about power." And to rework traditional power structures and roles in the classroom, we teachers must trouble our own impulses to enact the teacher role—the role that positions the teacher as the holder of knowledge, described by Freire (1970) as the banking approach to education, whereby knowledge is to be deposited in children's brains as money is in banks. To uphold the traditional "teacher" role is thus to enact an oppressive pedagogy (Freire, 1970), which disempowers and silences children, while communicating to them that they are not in charge and that the work of the classroom, of constructing curriculum, is not their work.

Figure 1.1. Critical Cycle

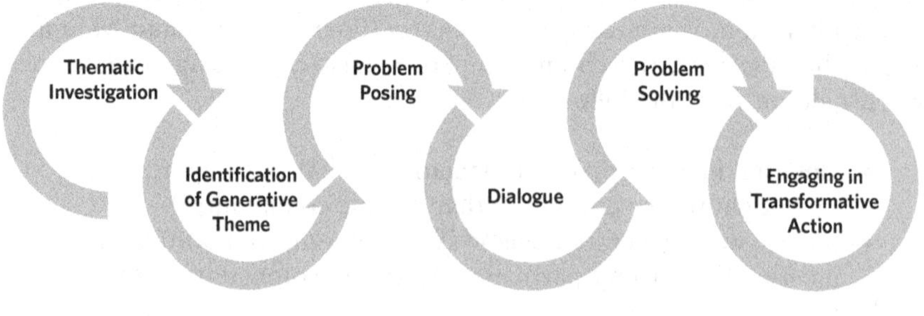

Adapted from Souto-Manning (2019). Reprinted with permission of Taylor & Francis Ltd.

This story, albeit seemingly small, is a reminder of how these tiny classroom moments, these stories that we allow to happen, can actually construct our classroom communities. This was a story about asking questions, identifying a problem, troubling the roots of the problem, listening to multiple stories, making choices for the class, and children taking on authority and ownership of their care for one another and for their classroom. This was the beginning, a tiny step into the complex conversations and critical thinking that Pre-K East would share as a community in the coming year. These small moments, when they are allowed to happen, lead to big curricula.

BUILDING BLOCKS FOR CONSTRUCTING LITERACY CURRICULA IN THE EARLY CHILDHOOD CLASSROOM

There are a few concepts that frame our thinking as educators when we build literacy curricula out of children's play. These are not structured, prescribed practices that you need to fully adopt in your classroom in order to do this work. These concepts are meant to be flexible; they are building blocks for constructing a way of thinking about children's thinking and work. We hope that you will take these building blocks and make them your own, that you will reshape and reinvent them. Find ways they can make sense in your own practice, in your own classroom world. After all, we understand that curriculum cannot be imported and exported; it must be reinvented (Freire, 1998).

We hope that you will use these practices in small ways and during seemingly small moments, like when there is a big water spill or a messy experiment with paint. Test out this thinking, these conversations, in small ways and see what emerges. Use these tools to build a practice that makes sense for and in your classroom.

These building blocks of classroom practice are particularly powerful because they offer an integrated approach to the curriculum. These practices transcend discrete skill sets or academic "subjects," focusing instead on critical thinking, discussion, questioning and problem solving across the curriculum. These ways of collectively thinking, coconstructing, and collaborating with children provide a broad view on thinking and learning, offering authentic connections that lead to an integrated curriculum.

The following sections contain explanations of the ways Dana makes sense of these building blocks in her classroom. It is important to understand that they are ever-changing with the children and in the world that we inhabit together. Yet, as they change, they also have a staunchness to them that supports Dana, her teaching, and her actions. This is especially the case in those moments when she wonders, worries, and questions. They stand behind her, reminding her of why she teaches, how she teaches, and what might be possible . . . and yet not quite realized.

The Emergent Curriculum

In the Pre-K East classroom, Dana uses something we call "the emergent curriculum." We use this name because the curriculum generates from young children's interests and priorities. It emerges from their questions. This means that the teachers do not have a binder filled with their "plan" for the year. That does not mean that Dana is without binders—never fear! She has a number of binders and checklists with the expectations for the year. There are mathematical, social, scientific, and literacy goals that must be achieved. She just does not know the path her classroom community will take to achieve them—until she meets the individuals and the community that make up the pre-K class that particular year. This is both the beauty and the anxiety of the emergent curriculum. Dana has a sense of where they are going. But as the year starts, she just does not yet know how they will get there. This practice requires that teachers listen to and learn from their students. Instead of a top-down approach to curriculum, one could say that this is a bottom-up approach. But we like to refer to it as a curriculum that centers children—who they are, what they are interested in, what they know, the questions they have—building bridges to the goals, which are enveloped by binders and formatted as checklists.

Each year presents a unique question (or a few of them), and new faces (in Dana's case, 16 of them) and the possibilities they will present. Their play, their interests, and their interactions will shape the paths that she takes. This approach is in stark contrast to approaches that center the goals to be achieved without considering the diversities and human beings that will populate the classroom. The Book Project, described in this book, is an example of this emergent work with children.

The use of an emergent curriculum requires reshaping our role as teachers. Listening becomes vital, because it is through listening that we support children in constructing the foundation of the curriculum (Rinaldi, 2006). We listen to their play. We watch and question their experiments. Sometimes, we let sand fill the sink and water run over, knowing that we can build curriculum from that moment. We learn to build, to coconstruct curriculum with the children. The coconstruction of curriculum requires a disruption of traditional notions of teacher and curriculum as static and all-powerful. We have to let that go. We have to relinquish our firm grip on those binders full of plans that, although well-developed, may not relate to the children—who they are, their interests, their priorities. Our careful teacher plans also may not relate to that moment in time, and the many meanings and experiences layered into each particular moment in history that we share with the children. These constructs are dissolved in favor of the fluidity of critical pedagogy in which "knowledge" and "curriculum" are spaces for questioning, problematizing, and meaning-making for children (Souto-Manning, 2010). This is that moment when you were going to make the rule—"No sand in the sink"—and instead you ask the question, "So, what should we do?" We teachers take a "humble stance" as participants and facilitators of discussion, but not as all-knowing (Freire, 1998; Souto-Manning et al., 2018). We acknowledge to the children and to ourselves that we do not hold all the answers. We will negotiate the answers as a class, as a new learning community. This reconceptualization of teacher and curriculum enables more complex, culturally situated meanings to emerge as the children engage collaboratively in critical work. This critical work is fostered within the context of culture circles (Freire, 1970; Souto-Manning, 2010, 2013).

Culture Circles

We began this chapter with the story of "The Great Sand and Water Catastrophe" because it demonstrates the very first steps into the work of culture circles in the early childhood classroom. Culture circles are the collaborative, critical space in which the children in this class come together to discuss their ideas, questions, and concerns (Freire, 1970). It is the space in which they simply learn to be and to evolve as a community. Within this space, they inquire, face questions and problems, and most important, listen and speak themselves into a classroom community. It is in this space that they become a community. It is in this space that this community creates, problematizes, builds, and resolves.

Culture circles are a careful pedagogical practice that teachers develop in collaboration with children; they are part of the classroom routines and expectations upon which a classroom community is founded. Culture circles serve as an apt framework, an essential space for our big questions, concerns, and issues as the year evolves. Yet a culture circle is not a space that a teacher can speak or command into existence. It is a space cocreated with care and thought, where children can engage in risk-taking and risky asking. It can only be made real through the participation and engagement of every member of the community, including, and especially, the teacher. Although it was a pedagogy originally developed within the context of adult education by Brazilian educational philosopher Paulo Freire (Souto-Manning, 2010), we have found that it serves as a powerful pedagogical space for young children's learning.

In "The Great Sand and Water Catastrophe," you can see the beginnings of this practice. The children step into the circle, expecting the teacher to play a punitive, authoritative role. They expect punishment and requirement from the teacher. Instead, they are met with questions. As a teacher, Dana is there. She is present, facilitating and providing necessary structure to support the children and their conversation. But the power and problem solving are turned back onto the children. In the story, you witness Susan calling Dana back to her expected role again and again. Again and again, the questions are turned back to the children, who offer their ideas with excitement, and eventually solve the problem.

This was a tiny culture circle, the first of the year. And it was about something so small, so tangible. Yet this tiny conversation encompassed big ideas. This story told the children:

- I (the teacher) do not have all the answers,
- I (the teacher) will not solve your problems for you,
- You (the children) have valuable answers,
- You (the children) are able to solve problems,
- We (the community) will listen to your ideas, and
- We (the community) will take your ideas seriously and practice them.

This small moment (and large mess) provided the very first step into the practice of culture circles in this classroom. The space that is created by this, and other conversations like it, is the space in which the children's literacy curricula will ultimately be built. Children who are savvy about this kind of talk are prepared for curricular work founded on their own ideas. They are prepared to problem-solve, to take their own and others' ideas seriously, and to take ownership and authorship of the shape of their learning.

Project Work

Dana and Lucinda engage with project work in the Pre-K East classroom to organize and make sense of the emergent curriculum, to document the learning that is unfolding in and as a result of children's questions and priorities. Project work—and its focus on listening and on documenting—provides a valuable framework. Combined with culture circles, it frames what we title "the emergent curriculum." That is, project work helps organize the listening and articulate the emergent curriculum. Though Dana takes inspiration and understanding from some specific research on the project approach (Helm & Katz, 2011) and the Reggio Emilia approach (Edwards, Gandini, & Forman, 2011), over the years, she has developed her own ways of organizing and making sense of project work that is meaningful in the classroom. That is, she has reinvented it in ways that make sense in her classroom. As you consider constructing your own child-centered literacy work in your classroom, we encourage you to do the same. Read about project work. Explore the resources out there. Use what you find useful and integrate from multiple resources in order to make the practice make sense.

The Book Project emerged from a class rich with storytelling in children's play and heavy with their knowledge of older siblings' "publishing parties" and "real writing." Dana and Lucinda listened to and documented themes and questions as they emerged in children's play and conversations.

The teachers then worked with the children to connect these themes and bring them together into a study and exploration of books as a whole.

When we think of emergent curriculum constructed at the intersection of culture circles and project work, we think of constellations. There are so many tiny stars in children's thinking. When we teachers practice emergent curriculum that documents children's wonderings and honors children's questions, we take note of those stars. We work with children to connect them, to see their relationship to one another, to coconstruct curriculum. Ultimately, the scattering of stars comes together in an image, a constellation that makes up the curriculum itself.

Here are some basic concepts about project work that Dana finds particularly useful in her practice, combined with advice for those considering engaging in such work:

- Projects are a way of making sense of children's collective interests.
  - Listen carefully to their play. When themes consistently emerge from multiple children over a sustained period of time, you often have the makings of a project.
- Although projects are based on children's ideas, it is the role of the teacher to help the children organize, collaborate, and make sense of the work.
  - Even as you give children the power of their own ideas, you are helping them to make this meaningful, to make it make sense.
- Projects foster children's academic development.
  - When considering a project, look carefully at the academic content knowledge and skills your students need to work on during the course of the year. How can these be integrated into this project? What skills and content knowledge could fit in? What skills and content knowledge will not fit in? Often, the necessary skills and content knowledge present themselves naturally as part of the work, but it is helpful to make a list and have a sense of how you might integrate them.
- Projects are cogenerated and codesigned by teachers and students.
  - Work with the children to clearly articulate a plan and associated goals. This typically occurs over many meeting times and may shift as children's investment in the work evolves. Keep asking them questions: Why? Why are we doing this? What do you want to do? Why should we do that? Yes, and . . . ?
- Projects are predicated on documentation.
  - You will need to have records of the children's words so that you can return to them, reference them, track their growth, and understand the growth of the project. Take notes, record with a phone, take pictures, find ways to document the process.

- Projects reposition children as problem-solvers and critical thinkers.
  - » Let the children solve the problems. Every project has problems. Zip lines get stuck in trees. Plaster hardens much faster than expected. People leave for summer vacation before work is shared. These problems are possibilities. They are the chance to lay it out for the children and say, "What can we do? How can we solve this?" Problems are a space for authentic critical thinking.

THE CLASSROOM AND ITS PRACTICES: CONCLUSION

As we conclude this chapter, we want to offer an important insight into the shape and perspective of this book. What we share in these pages are ideas about how curriculum is developed, how early literacy work unfolds. We share ideas about how things work, what some call theories. These theories generate from the everyday realities and experiences of Dana's pre-K teaching. Dana has been a teacher for over 17 years. She has taught in what some would label "ideal" or "easy" classrooms. She has also taught in places where she had to search through the garbage to gather supplies, and where at the end of the year she had nothing but dried-up markers and broken crayons. Dana has engaged these practices in a wide range of classrooms, shifting the practices to meet the realities of underresourced child care settings, with monolingual, bilingual, and multilingual children, in complex behavioral environments, and within inclusive pre-K classrooms. In each classroom community, the practices shift and take on new forms to meet the needs of the children and teachers of that place, that moment. The theories we offer came out of this pre-K classroom and the many other classrooms in which she has worked. They also are informed by the classrooms where Mariana taught—in Brazil and in the United States.

What we share is the story of one classroom, one year. Yet we also share the framework employed, the processes undertaken, and the connections to academic learning in hopes of shedding light on another context—the context where you teach, however similar or different it may appear from the Pre-K East classroom. We hope you will take these ideas into your mind and into your classroom community and see how they might make sense for you. Reinvent them and make them meaningful.

There are a few universals: Children are capable, they bring experiences with them, and they have questions. And we teachers have curricular goals to be met. Yet, with that in mind, please know that there are no rules for this kind of work—as long as the foundational commitments remain:

- Listen to and value children's questions.
- Create space for children to develop as critical questioners.

- Document the work, making clear connections between children's priorities and questions and curricular mandates.

Though there are key commitments, they will come to life differently in different contexts. Remember that there is no prescription for this work. Like all good teaching tools, these ideas are meant to be manipulated to support those of us who live the ever-changing life of classroom work.

We know that some of the stories we share here about Dana's teaching practices may sound idealized, contained within the neat and well-defined boundaries of school days. We recognize that it is easier to tell stories after they unfold, after the school year is ended. As they unfold, though, they often feel chaotic, like the story about the "Great Sand and Water Catastrophe," which spilled beyond the regular school day.

The Great Sand and Water Catastrophe (Continued)

Luckily, it was a half-day. As the children tumbled out of the classroom, exhausted by the energy and stress of these first days of school, I turned back to my damp and sandy classroom. "I'm glad that the facilities closet lock is broken, because this job is going to require the use of the big mop," I thought to myself as I yanked the door open and rolled out the yellow mop bucket. But as I began the glamorous job of sweeping and mopping . . . and sweeping and mopping, I smiled. "It was worth it," I thought as I slid the mop back and forth. "We're going to get there."

It is with great hope that we conclude this chapter with the conviction that you, along with Dana, will get there, too. On to the next chapter!

CHAPTER 2

Storying in Play

Investigating the Purpose of Authoring

"That's the Story We Were Making!"

Many months had passed since "The Great Sand and Water Catastrophe." We had discovered one another, and ourselves in relation to one another. We had slowly become a community, with all its connectedness and dysfunction. The shape of our days felt familiar in this cold month of February. We were secure in our expectations and in ourselves.

This was the fertile, confident ground in which new possibilities could grow. A much more effective clean-up process than our first had been accomplished, and we were assembled on the purple rug once again. All eyes were turned on me again, in expectation.

There was a "story" card on our schedule for this time, and the children looked closely, eyes searching for the book. No book was produced. I took a deep breath and began: "Once upon a time there were sharks in Big Blocks. They were mean and wanted to eat the people on the boat. I walked across a special bridge so that the sharks couldn't bite me. . . ."

"Hey, that's what we were playing!" shouted Marion.

"Shhh," I replied. "I'm not done with the story. Then the shark jumped up and bit me. I had a really big cut on my leg, and I wanted a Hello Kitty Band-Aid." The class nodded at these details.

"Then I was crying," I explained, "because I was a baby and I needed help. The big shark that bit me—"

"That was me!" announced Peter.

"He came and said, 'I'm actually a good shark and I didn't really hurt you. See, that's just a pretend boo-boo.'"

"I looked down, and he was right! It was pretend." The class smiled in shared understanding of the differences between real and pretend boo-boos.

"I still wanted a Band-Aid, and the baby shark said, 'Oh, I have one in my first-aid kit.' He gave it to me, and then I was all better. Then we played together in the baby shark pool, because I turned into a baby shark, too. The end."

"That's the story we were making!" said Margo.

"Yeah, but we didn't say, 'The end' in it. We kept playing 'til the bell rang," added Scott.

"It's not like a real story because it's just a game," declared Susan.

"But it is!" Marion argued, "because look. Dana said it during the 'story' card time. Look at the schedule."

They all looked. They were right. I told the story during the story card time. So maybe it could be a "real" story. . . .

MAKING SENSE OF PLAY-BASED AUTHORSHIP

There is a process to supporting children in finding "real" stories in their everyday play. Children are not socialized to see their play, or their knowledge, as "real" authoring or "real" work. The concepts of "schoolwork" are firmly disconnected from the children's sense of themselves in their play or their understandings of the complex narratives that they construct as authors through their play (Genishi & Dyson, 2009). In fact, they often enter pre-K with restrictive notions of authoring, with the idea that *authoring* is a synonym for *writing*. This is not something Dana teaches her students, but something they somehow already know. They have already been told that play is play, and authoring and writing are school-related endeavors. Children are socialized to see writing and authoring as solely within the purview of schooling, not play. Through this isolation of authorship to the realm of formal schooling, children are positioned as not yet ready, not yet capable—all while they are fashioning intricate stories in and through their play. Somehow, many educators have come to believe this myth, to buy into this restrictive notion of authorship.

As the stories that unfolded in Pre-K East over the course of a year were captured, recorded, and read, leading to the development of The Book Project, we realized that we had to share these stories in hopes that they could transform understandings of authoring. They certainly had transformed children's conceptualizations of authorship in Pre-K East, and we hoped that they could do so in other preschool and pre-K classrooms. We hoped they would serve as an antidote to the push-down of academics, often associated with the rhetoric of getting the most out of investments made in early education. We hoped they would unveil how, through play, children develop as authors, as composers, and as writers.

We believe that "professionally informed teaching decisions [must be] based on the data" collected in our classrooms, including the very important stories children coauthor as they play (Owocki & Goodman, 2002, p. 3). It is from this perspective and with this commitment that we embrace the idea that young children are "already ready" (Ray & Glover, 2008), that they enter the pre-K classroom as capable communicators and as apt authors. To communicate this belief, that young children are capable authors, Dana looked closely and listened carefully to the young children in her pre-K class, learning from and with them during play. She captured their stories as they were unveiled, writing them down without questioning their realness, editing their characters, or revising their novel plots, which often remixed settings, relationships, and possibilities. She simply recorded them.

In studying children, their stories, and authoring processes seriously, we were learning and "discovering not so much the limits and weaknesses of children but rather their surprising and extraordinary strengths and capabilities linked to an inexhaustible need for expression and realization" (Malaguzzi, 1998, p. 78). Through this process, we came to understand that:

> In order to participate fully in the life of this classroom, both teachers and children necessarily become authors of their own texts and audiences for other members of the community . . . [as] the most compelling and immediate reason to explore print or art was to gain access to classroom interaction. (Rowe, 1994, p. 191)

Thus, it is up to us as teachers to support young children in finding the path to see themselves as authors, to nurture them as authors, to cultivate their authorship. These talents—of authoring sophisticated plots with rich characters (Souto-Manning & Yoon, 2018), of weaving and making symbols (Dyson, 1990a)—are rich and fluid in children's play. After all, "play is an important vehicle for . . . promoting language, cognition, and social competence" (National Association for the Education of Young Children, 2009, p. 14). It is our role to lift the curtain on that authorship so that children can make the connection between the stories they author in play and the concept of authorship (orally and eventually in writing). Then they can rediscover their play, coming to understand play as a site for the development of their own stories. For this to happen, we must first understand that any text, oral or written, takes shape and makes meaning within social worlds (Dyson, 2008).

A Sociocultural View of Authorship

We subscribe to a sociocultural view of authorship, which is predicated on the understanding that "language in use and situational contexts are inseparable" (Dyson, 2008, p. 16). This reminds us why it is important to develop community (as Dana did in her pre-K class) before focusing on the development of authorship and on the weaving of symbols (Dyson, 1990b). This viewpoint also reminds us why is it essential to defend child-centered, make-believe play within the context of early childhood classrooms . . . for extended periods of time. The role of the teacher is not to tell children how to play, but to record, learn from, and (at times) help children extend their play. It is through play and through community that children develop the basics of authoring, which are "children's repertoire of human voices, their multiple symbolic tools, and their guiding communicative practices" (Dyson, 2008, p. 15).

If we are to support the development of young children as authors, we must "look and listen beyond the words on the page and thereby allow more of children's language, cultural and textual knowledge, and know-how to enter into and inform official efforts to help them compose" (Dyson, 2008, p. 14). But beyond allowing, we must cultivate and sponsor their literacy development in and through play. This was Dana's intention on that cold day in February on which the story that opens this chapter was told.

Although Dana has observed that the return to the classroom in January after winter break can harken back to the initial nervousness and fear of the first days of school, she has also watched as children find those fears quickly dispelled. Soon, they are confident and assertive in the spaces and relationships they have come to know so well. Year after year, Dana finds that there is a particular power in this time of the school year. The classroom community has been together for a long time. The learning community has been built through the sharing of successes and storms weathered together. As Dana explains, "There is a particular wisdom to my pre-K children in midwinter. The returning veterans after the winter break, they are amazed at their knowledge, at the distance they have traveled from those first days of school." And this is essential for authorship, for children's development as authors. It is during this time that we must consider "how we . . . might transform our teaching practices so that we may better build on, respond to, the diverse resources of our children" (Dyson, 2008, p. 14). During this powerful time, when the air is filled with sparks of connection and possibility, Dana and Lucinda took the next step, purposefully and intentionally sponsoring literacy in the Pre-K East classroom.

Early Childhood Teachers as Sponsors of Literacy

What exactly is the role of the teacher if not to facilitate learning and co-construct knowledge? We propose that teachers can be reconceptualized as "sponsors of literacy" (Brandt, 1998). But what are sponsors of literacy? Brandt (1998) described sponsors of literacy as "any agents, local or distant, concrete or abstract, who enable, support, teach, or model, as well as recruit, regulate, suppress, or withhold literacy" (p. 166). Such sponsorship is important for young children to develop as authors. After all, as Vygotsky (1978) wrote, "what a child can do with assistance today she will be able to do by herself tomorrow" (p. 87). And this assistance can take the form of sponsorship.

As Brandt (1998) explained, sponsors of literacy "are a tangible reminder that literacy learning throughout history has always required permission, sanction, assistance" (p. 167). This has been true with adults and is also true with young children. As sponsors of literacy, early childhood teachers "set the terms for access to literacy and wield powerful incentives" (pp. 166–167), such as sanctioning play as authorship. After all, literacy sponsors sanction spaces for literacy engagements, just as Dana does in her classroom. Such spaces, in the pre-K classroom, take the form of play: child-led, unstructured, make-believe play. It is in such spaces that young children negotiate their roles as coauthors and move toward the development of mastery. Although sponsors of literacy are often "more knowledgeable, and more entrenched than the sponsored, sponsors nevertheless enter a reciprocal relationship with those they underwrite. They lend their resources or credibility to the sponsored but also stand to gain benefits from their success" (p. 167).

As teacher-facilitators who regarded their students as capable authors and apt curriculum cogenerators, Dana and Lucinda took on the role of sponsors of literacy in the classroom. The teachers created spaces where authorship was sanctioned, socialized their students into the process and language of storying, ensured time for extended play, and held the space for discussions around literacy to happen. In doing so, they discussed their students' rich storytelling, noticed and noted sustained story themes—such as the sharks in the Big Blocks area—and the deft moves of collaborative composers, or story authors. The teachers also benefited from the development of the children as authors, meeting the expectations set forth by learning goals and standards, and the pressures (at times) imposed by parents and families who bring "a range of human relationships and ideological pressures . . . turn[ing] up at the scenes of literacy learning" (Brandt, 1998, p. 168).

In such a role, Dana considered: "How can we connect the children's play to their idea of themselves as authors?" She knew that her "recognition of the importance of continuities from oral into written language, and the connections between oral and written language, informs excellent teaching in many classrooms" (Lindfors, 2008, pp. 15–16). It was not a matter of imposing authorship onto children's play, but of helping them see the connections between their storying in play and what is deemed to be literacy in schools (as some of her students had pointed out), helping them reconceptualize authorship in ways that repositioned them capably and agentively.

UNDERSTANDING AUTHORSHIP IN THE PRE-K CLASSROOM

Recognizing the interconnections of reading and writing and of text and talk (Lindfors, 2008), Dana pondered how she could utilize the "official," established routines of the classroom to shift her students' understandings of authorship and of themselves as authors. She decided to draw on children's established reading or decoding routines to sanction official spaces for the recognition of their stories as authorship. One such official routine was the daily schedule.

Dana was always amazed by the power of the daily schedule posted on the board and the importance it held for the children. She knew that each and every year, her students referenced it constantly. This year was no different. Her students reveled in their ability to decode it, to read it. They checked in with their teachers if the schedule deviated even slightly. They were amazed when a new "schedule card" was revealed (when something "new" was added to the schedule). The routine of the schedule was somehow wrapped up in the children's wisdom of the classroom, in the journey they had traveled from being "the new kids in school" to the veterans of the winter months. The daily schedule was a space that housed their knowledge of the day, their expectations for the future, and their confidence in their authority and belonging in the classroom. In this official framework, one deemed important by the children, Dana chose to place their stories. It had meaning for them, and "meaning-orientation is such an essential part of the child's language experience from birth" (Lindfors, 2008, p. 45).

The idea of space is a complex one that we do not fully unveil or explain here. Yet we want to make visible three spatial perspectives conceptualized by Soja (1996), as they afford us understandings of ensuring that young children have space to enact stories, even in light of academic and standardization pressures. As Genishi and Dyson (2009) underscored, "we seem to be stuck in a time warp in which . . . standardization has become the 'fix'" (p. 10). Instead of regarding the reality of standardization or imagined practices as the only possibilities, Dana brings both of these perspectives together in the spatial perspective of her classroom. But what do we mean by spatial perspective?

According to Soja (1996), "a Firstspace perspective . . . focused on the 'real' material world" is in contrast to "a Secondspace perspective that interprets this reality through 'imagined' representations of spatiality." A Thirdspace perspective "can be described as a creative recombination and extension" (p. 6). This is the perspective we take in this book, reconciling and creatively recombining and extending real and imagined conceptualizations of young children as authors. But we are not the only ones who take a Thirdspace perspective; young children do, too, as they collaborate, cogenerate, and coauthor, remixing and extending their identities and practices.

In the Pre-K East classroom, young children's collaborations were essential to cogenerating curriculum (employing the framework presented in Chapter 1). They were also foundational to their coauthorship of stories within the context of child-centered and child-led play. So, to sanction a space for story, Dana had to locate it within the ethos of collaboration that characterized her classroom, and help children understand play as authoring without introducing adult constraints or impositions onto this sacred space.

The "Story Card": Sanctioning a Space for Story

The "story card" in the schedule had signaled the reading of a book. It told Dana and her pre-K students that a "real" story was about to be read. When the teachers placed a class-authored "story" into that framework, it ignited new possibilities and brought out powerful questions:

- Was this a real story?
- How did something get to be a real story?
- How could it be "The end" when the story was still being played out in the Big Blocks area?
- Would it be a story with chapters?
- How could a story become a book?

This small moment of story, connecting the children's play to the official "story" space of the classroom, opened up a new world of authorship for the class. It was as though something had been ignited in the children, something latent that they had known inside but had never connected before. Their worlds were full of stories. They were the authors of these stories. Now they had only to think about what the shape of that authorship might be.

It is important to note that the teachers and young children in this pre-K classroom were having discussions that are relatively new in the field of literacy education—new for adults who are members of this professional community and likely even newer to members of the society in which this pre-K is located. What we mean is that a few decades ago, the authoring done within the context of Pre-K East would not have been seen or understood as "real writing" or as "real authoring." As a result, this is a transformative action. Claiming the label of author and sanctioning spaces for stories in the pre-K classroom are powerful actions. They acknowledge and they name how children engage in storying long before they weave symbols on paper recognizable to adults as letters. This happens long before young children combine symbols to make words and combine words to make phrases. Yet, here we reaffirm that their process is real; it is real composing, real authoring.

On Make-Believe Play, Authorship, and the Development of Written Language

As Vygotsky (1978) underscored, we regard "make-believe play as a major contributor to the development of written language—a system of second order symbolism" (p. 110). In play, "representation of meaning initially arises as first-order symbolism" (p. 110). Then, it progresses to second-order symbolism (as we explore in subsequent chapters) when the children in Pre-K East coauthor books in what Dana titles The Book Project. This "second-order symbolism . . . gradually becomes direct symbolism. This means that written language consists of a system of signs that designate the sounds and words of spoken language, which, in turn, are signs for real entities and relations" (p. 106). With time, the "intermediate link, spoken language, disappears, and written language is converted [directly] into a system of signs" (p. 106). It is important for us educators to remember this. Just because writing is first-order symbolism for us adults, it does not mean that it is for young children. In fact, for them, oral language often serves a necessary link to the development of written language. As such, authoring stories in and through play is powerful to the development of writing for young children.

To support young children as they develop as writers, we must learn from them, coming to understand the function of particular symbols in their play (Vygotsky, 1978). Some of these symbols may be gestures, others may be words, and yet others may be objects. Thus, we must understand how children engage with "various forms of representation" (p. 111); there is no better place to do so than in play.

Play is thus a basic for the development of children as authors and their eventual development as writers. It offers fertile ground for the development of literate behaviors—of recognizing, decoding, or the writing of letters and words. Play is the language that connects, offering an integration of the curriculum itself before children have begun the process of (dis)integrating academic subjects (Bentley, 2013). Yet, it is important to understand that we are not advocating the development of one over the other. In reality, "these early literate behaviors will, over time, become more refined, precise, diverse, and conventional, as happens in oral language development as well. And, as with oral language development, collaboration—enabling partnerships—can play an important role in fostering literacy development" (Lindfors, 2008, p. 54). It takes time. It takes practice. This means that it is essential to make time for children to practice literacy in and through play. Play is a powerful site for children to develop as capable authors—at first using oral language, objects, and/or other symbols, and eventually bringing such expertise to the development of written stories.

CHAPTER 3

Investigating the Purposes of Writing and Publishing with Young Children

The story of the good/bad baby sharks ignited a frenzy of story writing and sharing in the Pre-K East classroom. Suddenly, every space was a space for story. Dana and Lucinda could not write fast enough, constantly being called to the unit block area, the Cozy Corner, and the sand table to scribe the many stories that were being authored within the context of the pre-K classroom. The idea of recording these stories seemed vital to the children, and with the children the teachers began to explore different techniques—from "invented spelling"[1] to Vivian Paley's (1990) storytelling and Augusto Boal's (1979) storyacting (adapted by Souto-Manning, 2013). (See also the discussion in Chapter 9 on the children's development of traditional literacy skills.) Each step served to further bring the children's authorship into that "official" space of "real" writing and "real" work. In this quest to make their work "real," the children proposed that they have a publishing party, "just like in 1st grade," as Clay, one of the pre-K students, suggested. Here is how our story unfolded. . . .

"Let's Have a Publishing Party!"

One day, we were meeting, looking closely at one another from across our circle, and thinking about our work. Clay, full of the authority of having three older brothers, announced: "We should have a publishing party! Just like my brother in 1st grade!"

This announcement sent a ripple of excitement through the classroom. A publishing party! Yes! They had heard of these things before. This reeked of official, 1st-grade work! We should have a publishing party.

1. "Understanding that letter patterns systematically relate to sound patterns is a major step toward being able to communicate through reading and writing. When children develop this understanding . . . they have developed the alphabetic principle, or have become alphabetic" (Owocki & Goodman, 2002, p. 81). Children who have become alphabetic invent spellings for words. Thus, "invented spelling" is an indication of knowledge about how reading and writing work.

As the conversation gained speed, I was filled with a sense of unease. This all seemed good, right? They wanted to have a publishing party. What a good goal. What a nice culmination to a project. I should be happy that this idea emerged, right? Yet something was not right. There was an artifice to the conversation. The children were carried by the enthusiasm of "big kid" work. And were they doing it with a sense of themselves as authors, or a sense of some incomprehensible symbol of "real" work?

But what were they *really* talking about? We needed to stop and think, to remember who we were, and why we were writing in the first place. We had the responsibility of troubling official conceptions and definitions of literacy, of authorship as the work of "big kids," as if it somehow had been missing from our pre-K classroom.

ON THE PRESSURE TO READ AND WRITE EARLIER AND EARLIER

In elementary schools, the youngest children often carry the burden of the "big kids" throughout their daily lives. No matter how early childhood teachers celebrate who they are, where they are right now, young children communicate that they know better. They are constantly faced with children who are bigger, faster, taller, and somehow "more" than what they are. They will never be fully convinced that they, in their totality, are the most, the best, the fullest. This is visible in the story that opens up this chapter, the story of how Clay, a young child in the Pre-K East classroom, expressed a wish to have a publishing party, "Just like my brother in 1st grade!"

Teachers feel this pressure, too. As Genishi and Dyson (2012) exposed, there is a "growing number of prekindergartens where teachers use worksheets to teach early literacy and math, as they try to respond to parental and societal pressure to 'educate.'" (p. 18). We don't believe that teachers choose these pressures. We believe that these pressures are imposed by a number of accountability measures, which purportedly serve to ensure that our children are learning—for example, benchmarks, assessments of progress, screenings, and imposed standards and goals—yet such pressures often end up comprising obstacles to their learning. This is part of the curricular battle we fight as teachers, as we harken back to the work of young children, the appropriate shape of that work, and the unique possibility that such work offers.

That is why, in this moment of "publishing party" excitement, Dana held back and thought again. She considered how the pressure to read and write earlier and earlier may have seeped into children's excitement to move from their storying through play in pre-K to 1st-grade publishing parties. This was perhaps, once again, their attempt to prove themselves bigger and "better." As Genishi and Dyson (2012) asked, "is racing toward reductionist benchmarks a worthy goal for the education of the very young? Is it an apt metaphor for the professional endeavors of skilled teachers? Is it, in the end, what we as a society want for our children—that they make a beeline for slim academic pickings?" (p. 18).

Dana asked herself: What was this *really* all about? Were traditional ideas and conceptualizations of authorship and writing seeping into her students' beliefs? And how could she honor children's walk toward their own goals, their own questions, rather than the artifice of the "real" work of the "big kids," somehow deemed to be better? Using this idea as the seed for investigation, or as a generative theme, the teachers and the children who comprised the pre-K learning community engaged in problematizing this suggestion, employing the framework detailed in Chapter 1. After all, Dana was committed to arguing "for shifting the spotlight from teachers straining to be accountable . . . [to] a change in the cast on the classroom stage, along with a change in scripts" (Genishi & Dyson, 2012, p. 18). In doing so, she embraced uncertainty and all its questions.

ASKING QUESTIONS: A PATHWAY FOR INVESTIGATING AND LEARNING

In Pre-K East, Dana begins this work by asking questions. After all, questions can offer a powerful pathway for investigating and learning, for inquiring into the unknown as well as troubling seemingly commonsensical assumptions. As a teacher committed to supporting her students' learning, Dana knew that "questions matter and will lead to an authentic and meaningful learning journey" (Souto-Manning, 2013, p. 39). In this case, there were questions that Dana asked herself and questions for the children to consider.

While it is important to honor students' questions, it is also important to create spaces where teachers can humbly share their own questions, stepping into the role of learner, constructing their own stories. Sometimes we educators silence our questions, under the assumption that only children's questions belong in the classroom, and in doing so, we silence stories. Yet, it is important to understand that when we teachers silence our questions, we compromise the learning process. And we compromise community. After all, we are not bringing ourselves authentically and fully into the classroom; nevertheless, we are expecting children to do so. As we wrote before:

> One of the hardest parts of this stance of silence is that young children are waiting for us teachers to tell them "What stories are school stories?" and "What stories are allowed at school?" When we shy away from a story, when we wait for the children, we teach through silence. (Bentley & Souto-Manning, 2018, p. 97)

So, while the obvious (and yes, easier) move would be to ask "Okay, class, what would we have to do so we can have a publishing party?" such a question would silence the story of who the children in Pre-K East already are as authors. It would silence their processes, their authorial expertise. In such a disempowering move, the teachers would then encourage their students to make books and have a celebration modeled after the 1st-grade publishing party. This did not resonate. It did not value children's processes. It did not honor who they were as authors. Most of all, it was not real for the kids. It had nothing to do with them.

Realizing that they had not answered the fundamental questions yet—the questions that would allow them to define authorship and publishing by and for themselves—on the following day, Dana gave continuation to their learning journey, sponsoring space for the continuation of the story that opened up this chapter. She utilized a common literacy structure, the morning message, which she wrote before students arrived, to be read at the start of the day. Dana's morning messages were written on a board in the meeting area; she often employed them to give continuation to the learning and questions posed in the previous day or week, as is the case in this example.

"Let's Have a Publishing Party!": Asking the Hard Questions

When the children arrived at school the next day, the morning message read:

Yesterday Clay said, "We should have a publishing party!" I am wondering:

- *Why do we have books?*
- *Why do we want to "publish" things?*
- *What does publishing do?*
- *What does publishing mean?*

During morning meeting, I used these questions to frame the conversation. There was a thoughtful, mind-churning hush as we processed these questions as a class. What was the point of a book, anyway? Had we ever asked ourselves that question?

Soon, hands were raised, and ideas poured out:

"Publishing means that they [our stories] can be sent and seen by people."

"We can have them on the bookshelf so that people can read them."

"Maybe we can write a new story that's about our class so the kids next year will know how to do the things that we do."

"We can put our books over in the Cozy Corner for the new kids. Then they can read them and know things that we did and that we know, even when we're gone in kindergarten."

"It's putting a cover on your book with a picture on it."

"It means to give books to other people."

When everyone seemed satisfied that this question had been answered, we moved on. "So, why is it important to publish books?" I asked.

The responses to this question were immediate. The kids were wrapped in the vortex of this investigation, digging deep into the whys and hows of what we do.

"So other people could read them."

"So you could sell them to the people that don't have any."

"Well, what if they don't have enough money?"

"Then you could give it to them. It doesn't matter about selling. It just matters that they read the book."

"So other people can read them and know things."

"So people can know stuff, like about making an airplane or about ninjas. If they read our books, then they can know. But they won't read it—I mean—they only read it if it's published."

This was one of our long morning meetings, one of those times when I glanced up at the clock with horror to realize that we were *really* late for P.E. That happens sometimes, you know? When you're so wrapped up in the now-ness of what is happening all other elements of the day get swept away. I gathered the kids up quickly, explaining,

"I am so sorry but we were so into what you were saying that we forgot about P.E.! We have to hurry!"

The kids smiled ruefully at the fallibility of their teachers. And maybe I was imagining it, but I could also detect a flicker of pride in the knowledge that their talk was so important that it swept away all thoughts of schedule and time from their teachers' minds.

After taking the children to the gym for P.E., Dana reflected:

> I will never cease to be amazed at the ability of children to distill the meaning of our work. How often do we forget to ask why we do what we do? How often do we go plowing into a new subject, a new skill, a new expectation without any sense of why it is essential or what purpose it might serve in the child's life?

Conversations such as the one above remind us educators to make space for questions in and through our teaching. And to ask genuine questions, questions we don't know the answers to—not guess-what-I'm-thinking kinds of questions. Ask why. Ask the children. Trust them and their capacity. It is from that "why" inquiry that real, deep, meaningful learning emerges. They need to know the point of what they are doing. Not only do they need to know the point, but they need to *make* the point, to construct their own understandings, to produce their own knowledges. The making of the point itself shifts the intrinsic motivation; it makes the purpose of the work about the children, rather than coming from an outside motivator. Education, then, no longer is preparation for life, for adulthood, for 1st grade. All of a sudden, education is harnessed as life itself . . . just as in the moment captured above in this morning meeting (Dewey, 1938).

This process, the asking of why, the children's construction of the purpose of the work, is also deeply related to the building of an integrated approach to the curriculum. When we consider integration, it is not about superficial connections or easy overlaps in subject matter. For this class, curricular integration is about something deeper; it is about stepping back and focusing on the essential components of the work itself:

- Why do we have books?
- Why should we "publish"?
- Why do we do what we do in school? What is the point?

When children are encouraged to take this broad view, to interrogate and make meaning about the essential elements of knowledge and communication, their understandings transcend divisions in curriculum. The answers to these questions about learning, authoring, and publishing relate to all elements of the curriculum, framing learning as an integrated whole.

As you consider the evolution of the lived story within the context of the Pre-K East classroom, it is important to note how that morning message served to encode children's voices. As individual children's voices were added to the morning message, they stopped being individual contributions and became collective messages to be read and rewritten in the life of the classroom. This was another small, but essential, step.

The morning message often constitutes an "official" space in the classroom (just like the schedule, which we explored in Chapter 2). It is a staple in early childhood and elementary literacy curricula; it can be used in other subjects as well. We propose that when we teachers bring the children's words and questions into these official spaces, we endow them with a sense of the official. When we offer teacher questions in these spaces, we unfix the static idea of the teacher as all-knowing. In these spaces, we can join young children as learners, as questioners, and open up the possibility of children as the holders and makers of answers.

YOUNG CHILDREN SPEAK, READ, AND AUTHOR WITH PURPOSE

Young children engage in story and expression with specific intentions (Lindfors, 2008; Rosenblatt, 1978). Young children's "oral language from birth carries out real communication purposes, and this can continue to be the case as the child learns to read and write" (Lindfors, 2008, p. 51). With this in mind, Dana knew that she wanted her students to author, to story, to use words, and not to simply learn how to spell words (Lindfors & Townsend, 1999).

Regarding her students as capable authors, in the Pre-K East classroom the mechanics of writing were not a priority or a precursor to authoring. They could not be. After all, the children were already storying in and through their play. They would surely learn the mechanics of writing in school, but first they needed to see themselves as capable authors. And they needed to regard the mechanics of writing as tools to communicate, to tell stories—not as the purpose of authoring or writing.

In this morning meeting, the children had a purpose—to define authorship, to understand the process of publishing and the purpose of books. Instead of taking 1st-grade meanings for granted, they constructed their own definitions. They established clear connections to authorship, to books, and to publishing. Collectively, the children interrogated the purpose of books, publishing, language, stories, and writing.

Through this conversation, the pre-K learning community had arrived at shared understandings of the purpose of their work, a purpose that guided their explorations of literacy as a class. These shared understandings were authentic to them. They allowed the children to establish a common purpose, being at the heart of the work they did. Further, they served as the starting point, unveiling the why of the work of authoring in pre-K and exposing the extensive knowledge that these 4- and 5-year-olds brought with them to the classroom.

Documenting What Children Already Know

As we think of pre-K, we often think about what we teachers need to introduce, to teach our young students. Yet the discussion above unveils how the children in Pre-K East brought sophisticated understandings of books and of reading. In fact, their comments captured much of what Marie Clay (2000) titled *Concepts About Print*. They showed clear understanding of the parts of the book (such as the cover). They understood that books contained stories and other kinds of information. They understood that publishing a book enabled others to read it. They also explained how one can learn (how to do) new things from reading books. Their comments signaled their understandings that a book has a front (a cover) and an author as well as how illustrations correspond to written text. And they also understood that publishing had been primarily a commercial endeavor (for instance, "So you could sell them to the people that don't have any").

Further, they understood how at times "we read to gain information, solve a problem, or carry out an action" (Lindfors, 2008, p. 18), with an orientation toward acquiring knowledge. Yet at other times, readers' "primary concern is what happens during the actual reading event" (Rosenblatt, 1978, p. 24), with an aesthetic orientation. "Sometimes you read for information *from* a text; sometimes you read for engagement *with* a text. Your *purpose* for reading influences your *way* of reading" (Lindfors, 2008, pp. 18–19).

Although it is impossible to unveil the entirety of the children's knowledge, it is easy to see how they brought sophisticated understandings of print and of reading to pre-K—or had developed these understandings in and through play, within the context of pre-K. Reassured of their knowledge and of the validity of their perspectives, the children in Pre-K East moved on to challenge themselves through writing, authorship, and publication; there was a meaning at the heart of the challenge. Whenever there was a struggle, they could look back to themselves, to their understandings, and know why. It was not because "my teacher told me to" or "because the publishing party is coming up," but because they made a choice to write. And writing had a purpose they recognized well—a purpose they had learned from social interactions with other children and adults. Writing was not an end, but a means for communicating and making sense in and of the world.

Together, the children developed a collective understanding of the need to be seen, to be heard, to share their knowledge, and to leave their trace. They understood how writing, how publishing could address such needs. Dana and Lucinda found that the children's collective perception of publishing as a space of long-term visibility and identity negotiation offered a powerful stance for the children. Not only were they empowered to challenge traditional schemas or symbols of books, but they were drawing on their knowledge, on one another's knowledge, to author themselves in the pre-K classroom. Through choice, time, and child-centered meaning-making processes, they created meaning and understanding collaboratively. They became a community of pre-K authors.

Writing, Authorship, and Publication

Actuating the belief that "all children can write," Donald Graves (1983) introduced the concept of "writing workshop." This approach "first emphasizes what children know, then the conventions that will help them share their meaning with others" (Graves, 1985, p. 36). As Graves underscored, teachers must believe that their students already know important things and bring rich experiences to the classroom. Then they need to work to communicate for the students the importance of their knowledges and experiences.

Graves (1985) detailed the following essentials to a successful writing-process program: "(1) adequate provision of time, (2) child choice of writing topic, (3) response to child meaning, and (4) establishment of a community of learners" (p. 36). Although this program has been adapted by many, taking on different forms and being comprised of different steps or components, we believe that the initial intention of the writing workshop is more closely aligned with the understanding that the process is more important than the product, that the development of authorship takes time, and that the process is likely to be unique for unique writers. Graves (1985) explained:

> Most teaching of writing is pointed toward . . . the mastery of minute, meaningless components that make little sense to the child . . . [and] rarely does it result in the child's use of writing as a tool for learning and enjoyment. . . . The writing-process approach . . . stresses meaning . . . then skills in the context of meaning. Learning how to respond to meaning and to understand what teachers need to see in texts takes much preparation. (p. 43)

For young authors, this means that the process of authoring and writing is multimodal (Wohlwend, 2013) and predicated on ownership, collectiveness, and support (Lindfors, 2008). Rereading Graves through the lenses of young children's language and literacy development, Wohlwend (2013) explored such a process, reframing writing workshops into a curricular framework entitled "literacy playshop." In the literacy playshop, young children (ages 3–8) are positioned as meaning-makers and creators of their own unique multimedia productions, instead of as being regarded as passive recipients of what is deemed official literacy knowledge. Also centering young children, Lindfors (2008) identified three concepts, which are key to guide the authorial process: (1) ownership, (2) community, and (3) guidance. We explain them below.

Within the context of the Pre-K East classroom, children's stories are authentic. Students own their stories. They are members of a community of authors; many of them interactionally coauthor through play. After all, it is through play that young children plan, map, draft, edit, revise, and perform stories. In Pre-K East, ownership means that the children own the story, that their voices are centered, and that they select and develop the topic(s) of the story. Community means that the authors are members of a supportive learning community and enjoy the support of its members, whether they are peers or teachers. Finally, guidance (conceived within the context of traditional writing workshops as conferencing, minilessons, and so on) becomes sponsorship. We propose that teachers who see children as competent authors and storytellers and work to cultivate their growth are de facto "sponsors of literacy" (Brandt, 1998).

"Let's Have a Publishing Party!": Asking the Hard Questions (Continued)

As the work continued, I wondered if the idea of the publishing party would emerge again. While I wanted to think carefully about the work itself, I did not want to deny the children's interests, if this felt to them like the culminating goal of the work. Somehow, the work had shifted, though. The classroom was humming with story, story performances, stories written on computers, stories scribed by teachers, and child-written stories with a variety of symbols, approximations of writing, and "invented spelling."

The children's questions and ideas were taking on sophistication as they began to consider their more informal writing (notes taken by teachers, labels placed on drawings) with the ideas of making "real" books and publication. We were entering new territory.

In the midst of this flurry of activity, I stopped to chat with Clay about his publishing party idea. I didn't want him to feel forgotten.

"Hey, Clay," I began, "I was wondering about the publishing party. Are you still thinking about that?"

Clay was busy illustrating an elaborate story entitled "Secret Spy Places" and looked up at me with a kind but harassed expression. "Nope. I'm too busy with writing the stories. It's kind of different from 1st grade, and we get to write more books than them anyway. They don't have time to do so many because they have to do math time and stuff."

He turned away from me. It seemed the issue was closed. I stood up and made to walk away, when I felt his powerful 5-year-old grasp on my arm.

"Dana, wait! 'Secret Spy Places' is almost done! Can I read it during the storytime on the purple carpet?" he asked urgently.

"Of course," I said, smiling, as we silently moved past the publishing party, and onto new things.

In this chapter, we sought to provide windows into how, as a class, the teachers and their pre-K students collectively interrogated the purpose of books, publishing, language, stories, and writing. Through conversations, they arrived at a shared understanding of the power of writing and of the purpose of writing. These coconstructed meanings supersede artificial subject-matter distinctions, drawing the curriculum together into an integrated whole. These negotiated understandings served as powerful tools for cogenerating a language arts curriculum. They served as the conceptual grounds on which The Book Project took root. The Book Project is the central focus of Part II.

Part II

"But How Can Our Stories Turn into a Book?"

Planning and Making

In the chapters in Part II, we examine the process of bookmaking as it evolved within the context of the Pre-K East classroom. Looking closely at classroom stories, we explore the ways in which the pre-K class collaborated to engage in an integrated process of authoring, book writing, and bookmaking. Using the children's words and the books they coauthored as our framework, we look at the children's ideas and the moves Dana made as a teacher, as well as the details and ideas behind the work. It is important to note that we do not present the work in this way for teachers (readers like you) to replicate. Instead, we seek to offer a map for understanding the development of The Book Project in the Pre-K East classroom.

Chapter 4 explores the evolution of The Book Project, attending to how the children provided leadership and detailing the questioning process in which the Pre-K East class engaged to make meaning around the work. In particular, this chapter focuses on the process of wondering and inquiry around the origin of stories. In doing so, it unveils how the teachers positioned culture circles as a space in which children wondered and questioned the emergence of stories, troubling commonplace assumptions regarding authorship and developing a stronger sense of their identities as authors.

Chapter 5 addresses the dynamic process of exploring texts with children. This inquiry process reveals the necessary elements children are expected to understand as they grasp early literacy, what Marie Clay (2000) entitled *Concepts About Print*. More importantly, it makes visible the elements of books that the young children in the Pre-K East classroom saw as essential and indicative of "real" or official books, revealing their existing knowledge about books and their own concepts about print.

As you will read in Chapters 6–8, this collaborative, child-centered project addressed a wide range of learning standards required of the pre-K curriculum in an authentic, emergent manner, employing the framework detailed in Chapter 1. Specifically, the books address mathematics and science (Chapter 6), language arts (Chapter 7), and social studies (Chapter 8) in ways that genuinely represent the interests and passions of this unique class.

We invite you to look at the stories, narratives, books, and quotes from young children's talk as a lens for exploring your own practice, drawing implications and exploring possibilities for your own class. Through our shared stories, we offer a process that can be meaningfully translated and thoughtfully reinvented across classrooms, schools, and communities. After all, the beauty of this work is that it as authentic, meaningful, and unique as classroom communities.

CHAPTER 4

Creative Writing and The Book Project

Young children come to school ready to tell, negotiate, and author complex stories. Many of them want to write, but are not sure how—and if—they can. It is thus important for teachers to create spaces for children's storylines and plots to develop in and through play (as explored in Chapter 2). It is important to center authenticity, choice, and purpose within a context filled with collectiveness and support (as explored in Chapter 3). It is also important to attend to young children's unique timelines for developing—as readers, as writers, as learners, and as individuals. While Dana "still want[ed] children to become readers, writers, and numerical problem solvers . . . academic purposes . . . [were] not at the top of a rigid schedule" (Genishi & Dyson, 2012, p. 19). The curriculum in Pre-K East followed children's interests, honored their experiences, and resulted from their questions.

In this chapter, we explore the process whereby the young children Dana taught in pre-K started to develop as book authors. This chapter starts with the story of how The Book Project was born in the larger Pre-K East community. Recognizing and creating spaces for the multiple interests and experiences of the young children she taught, Dana sought to honor individual children's timelines—as well as the timeline of the class as a collective. And thus, it wasn't until February that The Book Project began to develop. The seemingly simple conversation described below served as a pivotal point.

"Stories Come from Your Brain": *The Whole Pre-K East Book*

The story of "formal" writing and publishing in pre-K began with a seemingly simple effort. "We can just write a book with all of our stories in it! Then it can be *The Whole Pre-K East Book*," announced Alexander, a leader fond of simplicity and straightforwardness. All right, we all seemed to agree, we would write a book. Simple enough.

Yet the simple choice to "just write a book" didn't completely resonate. There seemed to be a layer missing, a part of the conversation that needed to happen first. And so, when the children arrived in the classroom the next day, they were met with the following morning message:

> *Good morning, Pre-K East! Yesterday we decided that we would like to write a book. It will have stories from everyone in it so it can be* The Whole Pre-K East Book. *Before we start working on the book, I was wondering:*
>
> - *Where do stories come from?*
> - *How will we get the stories for our book?*
> - *What do you think?*

The class, now in early winter and used to our morning routine, which included morning messages filled with questions, sat down for morning meeting and began to discuss the questions. Where did stories come from?

"From your brain," explained Margo. "You think about a story, and then you write it." Her comment was followed by lots of nods. That seemed an adequate answer to the question. But the children were far too accomplished at this type of discussion to let it go at that. More hands were raised, and we went on:

- They come from people who wrote them and people who want to make one.
- Stories come from authors who write books for children.
- You can get them from the library.
- How you can make a story is you can get a book and a piece of paper and you can copy some words from a book that was already made.
- You don't have to do exactly the same words as the first book, but you could do some of the words.
- You could get them out of books and you can get them out of stories that really happened. Like I wrote about the salamander.
- That's called nonfiction.
- My dad is writing a book about his life before I was born, so he's making the story about it.
- They make stories by writing the pictures in their mind.
- If you watch movies, you could draw what the movies look like. Like my sister drawed a Minion.
- The old-fashioned way of making those movies they had to make so many pictures and it took so long to make.
- Authors make books and publish them and that's how they make books.

The conversation slowly calmed as everyone felt their ideas had been represented. We were left with a wide array of possibilities for inspiration—some challenging, some as simple as sharing the storyline of a movie. With materials set up at the tables in the back of the classroom, several children elected to begin work on their writing. Others made other choices, heading off to the unit block area and the water table, but the topic of stories circled the room, popping up in the children's play.

We opened this chapter with this particular conversation because of the powerful effect that this culture circle had on the shape of The Book Project. When we think about doing this kind of critical work with children, we purposefully and intentionally undertake a process whereby we complicate the uncomplicated. That is, we trouble commonplace assumptions, problematize realities, and question certainty (Freire, 1970). For example, the idea of writing a book together seems just so simple. The skills, the process, the goal and its purposes—all seem so clear, and it is seductive to think of literacy working in that way. We can write the book and will have achieved our goals. Then the children will move forward on the path of literacy. But this perspective ignores all the underlying complexities inherent in this work. If you go the simple route, you miss all the good stuff. You will also impose adult assumptions of publishing onto children. They will become consumers of literacy, rather than developing as producers.

The complexities come out in culture circles (Freire, 1970; Souto-Manning, 2010) when we step past the obvious, the traditional guise of the language arts curriculum, and we ask questions. We problematize what we read in the world . . . instead of regarding realities as being unchangeable. We ask questions such as these:

- Why should we make a book?
- Where do the stories come from?
- What do we think about that?

It may appear that we are complicating things. Yet, asking questions like these and engaging in critical conversations with children are essential steps toward making visible the complexities that lurk beneath the surface of things—aspects that otherwise might seem simple, straightforward, and commonsensical. Through this process, we teach the children to challenge us, to confront injustices in the curriculum, to ask why, and, possibly, to reject what is presented to them. We create spaces whereby they are empowered to foster transformation.

WHAT THE CHILDREN ALREADY KNEW ABOUT BOOKS AND STORIES

Although we may be particularly pleased and impressed by comments like "Stories come from your brain" or "They make stories by writing the pictures in their mind," Dana and Lucinda knew that these words were not going to be the access point for all the children in the pre-K classroom. Not all of the children were ready to peer into the dimensions of their own brains, seeking the stories they knew were lurking there. Some of the pre-K students needed more concreteness in order to understand and connect with the origin of stories. Without the connection between the abstract and the concrete reality of a story, authorship would seem inaccessible. And luckily, all the teachers needed to do was to listen to the children—to the answers they offered. Their very comments afforded and offered other entryways and opened up possibilities for engagement. They brought so much knowledge to the classroom.

As the young children in Pre-K East offered their rich and varied ideas about where stories come from, they also made visible what they already knew about stories, books, and how print works. For example, the children in Dana's pre-K class had expressed that authors write stories (for example, "They come from people who wrote them and people who want to make one") and that books were authored with particular audiences in mind (for instance, "Stories come from authors who write books for children"). The children understood that books could be purchased or acquired from libraries. Further, they saw themselves as authors and knew that published books could serve as mentor texts for the development of their own books (for example, "How you can make a story is you can get a book and a piece of paper and you can copy some words from a book that was already made"). They understood the possibility of story adaptations and also communicated how books can serve as resources for verifying how words are written ("You don't have to do exactly the same words as the first book, but you could do some of the words"). They knew that some books were about real topics—"stories that really happened" ("Like I wrote about the salamander")—and that such stories were "called nonfiction."

The children who were members of the Pre-K East communities knew that authors can take inspiration from other books and make their own changes, and so could they. They shared how authors can get ideas from a movie, perhaps getting inspiration from a much-beloved Minion. Most important, they knew that "Authors make books and publish them and that's how they make books," and they knew that they, too, wanted to and could be authors. The idea of nonfiction and biography (how one of the parents was writing about his life) was introduced in this conversation. These concepts quickly gained traction as children offered their own real stories as potential topics for writing. They knew that they had real stories to tell—and they wanted to write them.

This conversation opened up the possibility for all of the kids to work collectively, on the same project. People often ask Dana how she differentiates curriculum through projects. The conversation shared above can be seen as differentiation at its best, and this differentiation is not even being executed by the teacher. Instead of thinking of differentiation, we invite you to think about how cogenerated curriculum can be universally designed to entail multiple forms of representation, engagement, and expression. This is what is often titled a "Universal Design for Learning," or UDL for short. It entails presenting content in different ways and from different perspectives, differentiating how students can express their knowledge, and exploring the why, the purpose of learning (National Center on Universal Design for Learning, 2012). It is best done, we think, collectively with children. After all, it is the children who are offering different paths into the curriculum, the children who are seeing the wide range of stories available to them and assessing the validity of all these choices. When we create a space for these conversations to happen and support young children in engaging around these kinds of questions, the curriculum opens up with diverse possibilities, representing the varied literacies they see in their own lives and that are present in their worlds.

THE AUTHORING PROCESS: WRITING *THE WHOLE PRE-K EAST BOOK*

The Whole Pre-K East Book (the first book published as part of what we came to call The Book Project) would prove to be the most straightforward of the books written that semester. The children each composed the draft of a story, illustrated it, shared their draft with the class, took questions and comments, received feedback from their peers, made edits, revised their original draft, and the book was published. This process deviated from some expected norms around authorship, as most of the children did not yet write the words for their stories (although some children did sound out words and write them when they chose). Instead, the teachers worked collaboratively with children, scribing stories either on paper or on the computer. As the teachers collaborated with the children, they asked questions:

- Did I get this right?
- Let me read this back to you. Is this how it should go?
- What will happen next?
- How do you want your story to end?

Through this collaborative process, teachers were able to support the children in thinking through the dynamics of their stories while always honoring the children as the authors who knew how to make the story "right." These stories then came to our circle during the official "storytime" and were read (often by the teachers, but sometimes by children). Children took questions and comments from peers regarding the stories, and these comments were used as a foundation for collaborative editing with teachers. After each child had the opportunity to engage in this process, the stories were combined to create *The Whole Pre-K East Book*.

The creation of these first stories very much followed the phases typically associated with the writing workshop. Yet it was not a process that

Dana imposed. This process (of going from drafting to publishing, venturing into the familiarity of editing and revising, ever-present in elementary classrooms) was born out of children's discussions of how they should approach the authoring of their very first book as a class. They knew that they needed to write down their stories (so they would remember them) and wanted to share their stories in class before sharing it "with the world." As was customary in the class, after listening to their stories, the children offered comments and asked questions as their peers shared, engaging in an *in vivo* peer review process akin to those experienced by published professional authors. Then, considering comments and questions offered, the children changed their stories to "make them better."

Although the process appears simple and all too familiar, the way Dana and her pre-K students approached this work as a class was where the complexity lived. Through the process of writing their book, they asked big questions about the origins of stories, where inspiration came from, the metacognitive process of thinking about our writing brains. They also discussed at length what was necessary to become an author. The process was rife with the sense of something filling up with meaning. Initially, we were presented with something simple, and almost embarked on a journey that had been crafted elsewhere. It was, after all, something that sounded like "great curriculum." Yet, as Dana recognized, "it had a hollowness to it." It felt aseptic, almost prescriptive. She pondered: What was it all about? Through discussions about the varied origins of ideas and the births of stories, that hollowness became full. It was no longer an aseptic undertaking, but a process filled with meaning and with the urgency of telling unique stories of who the children were individually and how, together, they comprised a community, the pre-K class. This created a foundation upon which the children's writing could be built, a foundation full of intention and meaning (Lindfors, 2008) that was created by the children.

The pre-K resolve resulting from the culture circle discussion led to great stamina. The children went to the table to author and, at times, write. Voracious pre-K authors had authored, revised, and then asked to write extra stories for the book. Their lack of experience did not matter. They had a variety of materials and media available to them, thus ensuring choice. They were members of a community that provided scaffolding and even wrote themselves into one another's stories. As teachers, Dana and Lucinda sponsored literacy, by creating the space, dedicating the time, and allocating the tools and supports needed. Over the course of a week, the more comfortable (and perhaps experienced) writers had taken a break from other activities and had written their stories with enthusiasm. Even Dana's more reticent writers had authored their stories, working closely with teachers, and through questions and scaffolding, writing their stories as well. Except for Ella . . . until she realized the possibility of coauthorship.

"Stories Come from Your Brain": *The Whole Pre-K East Book* (Continued)

The initial excitement of writers rushing to the table had dissipated over the week. I was on the last round of "I don't know what to do." This is a hard one for me, as I literally see stories leaping out of their lives everywhere we go. It's hard for me to imagine that they cannot see that, but here Ella and I sat, looking for her story.

"I don't knooooow," she wailed, sliding halfway off her seat like a noodle while twirling her hair. With Ella, there's usually a lot of flailing involved. The odd thing is that Ella is a consummate story-maker. On her own, with friends, with toys, and in dramatic play, Ella is always making a new story, full of drama and flair. She is sought out by classmates for just this skill. Yet, at this moment, seated at the table, her story was lost to her.

"Hmmm," I said, "Didn't you just do a story about Barbie?" You must know I'm really struggling if I'm referencing Barbie, but I was desperate.

Rachel happened to be walking by just as I mentioned the Barbie story. Just as Ella let out another, "I don't knooooow!" wail, Rachel stepped in and said, "Oh, yeah! That was really fun. I want to play that again. Remember, you were being Barbie?" Ella straightened up at her friend's enthusiasm, and pulled her torso from under the table, under which it had apparently melted.

"And we were going to the beach!" added Ella. We were saved; I began to type. "So what happened next?" I asked her, desperate to get this down on paper. But Ella was not so quickly deceived. Silence loomed again, and her body once more began to slide downward. Determined to save the moment, I asked, "Do you all want to write this together? Like, as coauthors?"

Ella's interested piqued again. "Can you do that?"

"Of course!" I cried, gratefully grabbing a copy of *The Napping House* from my bookshelf to show her. After all, it had been coauthored. This was my attempt to show her that if "real" published books had been coauthored, then our book, and her story, could, too.

"Okay!" said Rachel, always happy to take charge and help her teacher, who clearly did not have control of the situation.

What followed was the story "Get Back Rain," full of Barbie, beaches, rain, and boyfriends spraying them with the hose. It perhaps would not have been my choice of topics, but it brought Ella into the process, shining a light on her work as an author.

Rachel and Ella designed the illustrations together, and Ella insisted that both of their pictures be included as well as their names, which needed to be listed on the page as "the coauthors" (see Figure 4.1).

Figure 4.1. Coauthored Story

THE BOOK PROJECT: CHILDREN AS AUTHORS, PLAY AS AUTHORSHIP

The Book Project was based on Dana's and Lucinda's desire for the children to see themselves as authors and to understand their play as authorship. It seemed so obvious that they were authors, that their natural storytelling was authorship. Yet the teachers found that the formal structures and expectations of what "real writing" looks like had been stolen away from children, pulling them down a path where they could not see and access concepts and skills they already had. They knew how to tell stories. They lived stories every day through play. But once those stories were relocated away from the safety and creativity of play and into the risk of a blank page, somehow the children felt inexperienced, incapable, and not knowledgeable.

Through the process of authoring *The Whole Pre-K East Book*, the teachers were able to communicate to the children that they were knowledgeable authors. And the children were able to experience the process whereby, through what Vygotsky (1978) called second-order symbolism, their actions were imprinted on the pages of a class book. As Meier (2004) explained:

> Second-order symbolism refers to language as a symbol or representation of something two steps away from the real thing. For example, when children read and write the words *dog* and *cat*, they use the names of the animals (the words *dog* and *cat*) *and* the written symbols d-o-g and c-a-t to denote the real animals. Reading and writing dog and cat, then, involve a second-order of twice-removed level of symbolization. (p. 83)

In this first book, connections to the children's types of storytelling and authorship in daily life were fused. For Ella, it was the discovery of her Barbie dramatic play as story. Ella came to understand how the compelling stories that she authored for and with her friends in the dramatic play area were, in fact, stories. As such, they could be committed to paper and "published" as a part of our work. For other children, their stories lived in different parts of their play. For Marcus, it was the recreation of extreme

Figure 4.2. Marcus's Story

Snee Boarding in Vermont
By Marcus

In Vermont we go Snee Boarding behind a four wheeler. We hook a sled to the 4 wheeler, put a helmet on our heads, turn on the four wheeler and go over bumps! We built a big jump! When we fall, we sometimes get snow in our face, so we go inside to warm up and drink hot chocolate. We all go snee boarding again until we get cold.

The End

winter sports he played with his family. These memories, brought to life in his classroom demonstrations, became his story (see Figure 4.2).

For Emory, it was the combination of fiction and nonfiction in her dreams about an upcoming family wedding in which she would be the bridesmaid (see Figure 4.3).

All of these stories, real and fictional, were alive in the Pre-K East classroom, told in play, at the lunch table, and over the zooming of trucks at the sand table. The stories were alive and well. Dana simply had to work with the children to establish connections between these natural storytellings and their idea of themselves as authors. After all, initially, the children had seen play and authorship as separate endeavors.

The process of authoring *The Whole Pre-K East Book* also opened up the idea that there were different ways to author a story (as in the

Figure 4.3. Emory's Story

coauthoring of Rachel and Ella's story). Some stories were authored independently, some with coauthors. Seeing evidence of this in published, commercially produced books as well as in stories authored within their pre-K classroom, the children in Dana's classroom decided that there would be no "rules" for how they would author in their class. They regarded choice as key. In fact, the initial coauthored piece by the two girls (refer to Figure 4.1) opened up the possibility of more collaborative work in pre-K, some of which had lots of authors.

The Whole Pre-K East Book was the first book coauthored by the Pre-K East class. It was comprised primarily of separate stories with different authors. Yet it opened up the pathway for new ideas as the teachers and the children tested what was possible, considered and reconsidered their beliefs about authoring, and further explored the ideas behind authorship and publication. The first attempt was a simple book, printed on the copier at school and stapled together with the children in the classroom. It was through these first steps that they developed a foundation for the later works they would author as a class. Some of these are explored in Chapters 6–8. But before turning to other books, we turn back to the children in Dana's classroom as they shared stories from their first published book and unveiled the importance of community in growing a community of authors.

"Whee! Wheee! Whoaaaa!" And the Power of Classroom Rallying Cries

Stephan sat in front of the class, reading his story about skiing with his family (see Figure 4.4). "Then she fell," he said, with dramatic flair. "My brother went 'Whee! Wheee! Whoaaaa!' . . . and then he fell."

The class burst into laughter, and we were lost to any questions or comments that were meant to come after. When the giggling turned into a tumbling mass of kids on the purple carpet, I knew it was time to call it quits, and we headed out to the playground.

"That was a good story!" said Clay, still chuckling as he and Stephan went to pick up a basketball.

"Whee! Wheee! Whoaaaa!" became a common cry in our classroom, sort of like a class inside joke.

It is amazing to me how these little things draw us together, make us one unit, one community. There is none of the exclusive meanness that you might feel in edgy social dynamics. It's just that "You were there. I was there. We know this together. This makes us laugh, and no one else gets it" feeling that makes it safe to tell your stories and share of yourself with these people. Because these are your people. And when you yell, "Whee! Wheee! Whoaaaa!" we will burst out laughing. And no one else will know why.

But it doesn't matter. After all, there are always stories that make it onto the page of a published book as well as unpublished stories. This is one of those important, albeit unpublished, stories of solidarity, community, and humanity—all of which are at the very heart of stories, of authoring, and of publishing.

Figure 4.4. Whee! Wheee! Whoaaaa!

CHAPTER 5

Investigating the Body of the Book

Unveiling Children's Knowledge About Books and About Print

"But How Can We Make Them Be Real?"

It was early Monday morning in the Pre-K East classroom, which means that we were overflowing with energy and looking for the path we might follow through the coming week. Once again, we gathered on the purple carpet, chatting with one another and looking at our work. Lucinda was reading "Bad Stuff," a new title in our collection, authored by Peter. Peter's story was handwritten (by a teacher), on a piece of paper, and had a series of dynamic drawings beneath the written words. We were on a roll with this writing stuff, and I must admit, I was feeling pretty good about myself as a teacher. We really had this authoring thing down.

The kids were developing, performing, authoring, and writing stories all over the classroom, new work was emerging all the time, and the momentum had sustained itself for over a month now. We were moving right along. It's always in these moments of self-satisfaction that you know you are headed for a crash, and thus it was on this Monday morning.

As we finished reading Peter's story, he sat before the class prepared to take comments and questions. "Okay, everyone," I said, "comments or questions about Peter's book?" I was startled by the silence that followed. Everyone seemed very excited about the story itself, and it contained all the drama and violence that usually brought forth much commentary.

What had gone wrong? I looked to Peter's face, concerned that his feelings were hurt, but he had the same expression as the rest of his classmates. It was the "Whoa, my teacher needs some help here . . ." look. I waited as a hand finally raised. "Yes, Clay?" Peter acknowledged.

"So, I love the story. Especially the evil baby part. But . . . well, it's not a book yet," Clay said, looking quickly up at Peter and then me. Clay hates to hurt anyone's feelings.

I almost jumped in to stop him right there. Not a book? What did he mean that it was not a book? Was he saying that Peter wasn't an author? But I didn't get a chance to interject, because Peter quickly jumped in.

"Nope, of course it's not! It didn't get published yet. We have to publish it first so that it can be a real book." Peter looked back at me to make sure I was getting this.

"But how can we make them be real?" asked Susan.

"Maybe you need to write this down in your computer," Peter added.

And we were off, headed in a new direction as the children brainstormed about what turns a mere "story" into a "real book."

HONORING CHILDREN'S CONCEPTUALIZATION OF PUBLISHING

Young children will continually bring us back to the heart of the curriculum if the shape, the structure, of our classroom practice allows them to do so, if they are positioned as curriculum codesigners. In the above story, you see how the children in Pre-K East are adept at working within a culture circle framework (explored in Chapter 1). They are using some traditional ways of sharing their work, taking questions and comments, and carefully critiquing one another. But if you look closely, or delve beneath the surface, you will see how there are critical elements to the shape of the conversation.

The first critical element is children's stance, as is visible in their questions. That is, the children feel empowered to question Dana's expectations and assertions in the pre-K classroom. As you can see, although Dana had referred to Peter's work as a "book," the children did not give her the power to create that definition for them. They kindly, but assertively, spoke back against the construct that she offered, offering their own perspectives on what a book should be. Although this may seem small, this ability to interrogate purported truths and to problematize realities (what *is*) leads to in-depth learning. Through such problematizations, the children were asking themselves: "What makes a book, a book?" and "What does that mean?" They then proceed to make meaning as a class, collectively. They weren't going to accept that just because some adult decided that the act of sharing their work served as a proxy for publishing, that it did in effect. They pushed back. After all, what Peter presented did not look like a book or smell like a book. According to the children, it was not a real book. It did not look like the books they had read in their classroom, encountered in the public library, or treasured in the comfort of their homes.

Through this process of critically questioning commonplace definitions ingrained in traditional approaches to early literacy (and to the teaching of writing), it became clear how, for the children in Pre-K East, the idea of a book and the meaning around this symbol was deep and powerful. It could not be reduced to a number of pages with symbols on them stapled together. It didn't matter if Dana said so. This was because the children had developed their own conceptualization of what counted as a book.

Just like infants and toddlers learn to differentiate a car (a word often used to mean any sort of transportation, including a truck, airplane, and train) from other modes of transportation, the children in Pre-K East had learned to differentiate stapled paper from real books. This did not happen in a vacuum. It was a result of their prior experiences. That is, together, as a community, they drew on their experiences with books and they developed a typology of what counted as a book and what didn't. Peter's "book" didn't quite fit their definition. And they weren't going to pretend it did. Otherwise, they would compromise the authenticity of their work and instead embrace a pedagogical definition of a book (Lindfors, 2008). From their perspective, it would not be serving a real language/communication purpose. It was not that they did not know the parts of a book—its front and back, its title, its text, where it began, its message (conveyed through print and illustrated by pictures), or its directionality (Clay, 2000). They did. They had all these concepts about print, deemed important for the development of literacy (Clay, 2000). Yet, to them, the way a book looked and smelled, its material and binding, were key features in determining whether it was really a book. As a result, while the children in Pre-K East understood that stapled pages filled with symbols contained stories and carried meaning, they were simply deemed inauthentic as books.

Together, the children in Pre-K East had conceptualized publishing a particular way, drawing on their prior experiences. They had come to agree on what counted as a book. And as Lindfors (2008) reminds us, it is important for us to think deeply about the authenticity of materials with our students and carefully consider implications for literacy teaching and learning. It is also important to realize that no two classrooms would make the same choice(s) and determination(s) regarding the authenticity of a particular material. In sharing this, we want to press the importance of taking authenticity into account as you make decisions within the context of your own classroom and also unveil how the very concept of authenticity is context-specific and cultural. After all, the books Mariana grew up reading in Brazil looked and smelled very different from the books familiar to the children in Dana's classroom. Thus, cultural referents impact authenticity.

The questions—What is a book? What does that mean to me? and What does it mean to our community?—were essential for the children, not only because they established a common understanding within the context of the pre-K classroom, but also because they served as vehicles for the young children to engage in developing the notion that asking questions and developing meanings is their right, an essential part of their schooling process. This is the kind of critical thinking that can emerge through the foundation and use of culture circles in the early childhood classroom . . . even—and especially—in a classroom where the curriculum is emergent. After all, an emergent curriculum does not mean that anything goes. It must be developed within a purposeful and intentional framework. In the Pre-K East classroom, this framework was culture circles. Two other important elements to observe in the above conversation are the roles of the teacher and the curriculum, both of which traditionally stand like monoliths—static and unmoving, holding and yielding power. These are briefly discussed below.

RETHINKING THE ROLES OF THE TEACHER AND THE CURRICULUM

Moving into this kind of coconstructed curriculum with children, we teachers have to be willing to quiet some of that need for teacher-directed power and order in the classroom. How much more powerful might it be to support the children as they reveal the world to themselves? In order to participate in this process, we have to let go of a particular kind of power, and we have to "unfix" our curriculum. In that moment of satisfaction, of delighted teacher everything-is-going-as-planned-ness, we have to take a deep breath and let go of what we expected: let go not only of today, but also memories of when we ourselves were children in classrooms where the roles of teachers and curriculum were static. We must let go of the expectations we had when we entered teacher education programs hoping to develop as consummate teachers, and/or when we entered the profession hoping that the children we taught wouldn't find out we did not know everything about everything, especially everything about teaching. We have to let go and take that step forward with the children; so much becomes possible as we coconstruct a new curriculum *with* young children.

As a teacher, Dana embraced a fluid role of teacher and learner. Breaking away from the expectation that she held knowledge that must be passed on, transferred to her students, she purposefully made her thought process visible through "think-alouds." A "think-aloud" (Wilhelm, 2001) is a strategy commonly employed in the teaching of literacy to "enhance children's comprehension monitoring abilities" (Baumann, Jones, & Seifert-Kessell, 1993, p. 184). In "think-alouds," teachers orally describe some of the behaviors in which readers and writers engage, making visible questions they themselves consider and thereby modeling often "invisible" processes for learners. Although not always directly visible in the narratives, Dana consistently asked questions that made her own thinking visible, in morning messages, during meeting times, and in more fluid conversations in the flow of the classroom day. As we prioritize the children's voices in the context of this book, the teacher voice of think-alouds (Baumann et al., 1993) is not always visible, but this practice was an essential one as Dana worked to coconstruct curricula with the children.

"But How Do We Make Them Be Real?": Teacher Reflections and Rethinking the Plan

I was thrown by our last discussion. My hope as we worked together on this project was for the children to take control of the idea of authorship, to see these informal stories as authorings. Clearly, the children had a different perspective; I needed to find a new space to process and to hear them.

In need of answers, I began as I often do, cuddled up with a small group of children during our informal "working time," in what we call the Cozy Corner (our classroom library). These conversations are different, happening as they do in the flow of play, with children able to step in and out as needed. As we sat, looking at books and chatting, I took time to share some of my feelings with the children. I wanted to hear what they might say in reply.

"I'm worried today," I shared. Dominique, empathetic to her teacher, immediately tucked closer to my body. "Why?" she asked with concern, and Simon drew nearer. The idea of his teacher's vulnerability was intriguing.

"Well, I thought that 'Bad Stuff' was a book. I really wanted it to be a book, because I guess I want us to make so many books together. I was going to tell everyone that it was Peter's book. But remember during meeting?"

Simon and Dominique, quickly joined by Clay, nodded their heads.

"Some people thought it wasn't a book yet," I continued, "and now I'm feeling confused. I'm not sure what will happen next with our Book Project. And that's tricky for me. I really like to know what is going to happen next."

This was followed by a great deal of nodding; wanting to know what comes next is something that we all share. Cozy, confidential discussions like this allowed me to articulate my own hopes as a member of our community and to adjust them with the children.

In the above narrative, and the narrative that follows, Dana made visible her wonderings, expectations, and questions to her students. She explained the language she used. She also shared with the children the things she had wanted to say, but did not. In doing so, she modeled vulnerability and offered her students a window into her metacognitive process, displaying an awareness of her own knowledge about what teaching is and ought to be . . . then questioning traditional roles associated with teachers and deconstructing oppressive classroom and pedagogical structures. As Adichie (2009) explained, the trouble, or the danger, of single stories is not that they are untrue, but that they foster stereotypes. In making her process visible, Dana was troubling the "single story" of the teacher as all-knower and always certain—a historically sedimented stereotype that continues to permeate the profession (or at least impressions of the profession) today.

And just in case you were wondering, this is not an easy thing. In rethinking her own role as a teacher, at times, Dana wondered: "Am I a 'bad' teacher?" Because the prototypical "good" teacher stands at the front of the room, keeps kids quiet, and slowly reveals the world of knowledge to them. At least that was the kind of "good teacher" image that had permeated the literature, of "teacher as stranger" (Greene, 1973). Instead, Dana embraced the roles of teacher as learner and of teacher as cultural worker, documenting the children's cultural practices and centering them in her teaching (Freire, 1998). Taking such a perspective afforded Dana the possibility of coconstructing curriculum with the children she taught.

In Pre-K East, the curriculum was fluid and ever-evolving to meet the needs and address the questions posed by members of the classroom community. Dana, Lucinda, and their students cogenerated the curriculum, employing a culture circles framework (see Chapter 1). There was nothing monolithic about it. The curriculum coconstructed within the context of Pre-K East was multivoiced and considered multiple perspectives. It was filled with important, pressing questions. To be sure, it addressed mandated learning goals, but in a way that centered children's priorities. It was not as straightforward as moving through a pacing guide, but it was much more meaningful. Through the vignettes we share in this book, such as the one below, which gives continuation to the discussion presented earlier in this chapter, you can see how invested the children were—as experienced producers of knowledge, as agents of change, and as curriculum coconstructors.

"But How Can We Make Them Be Real?": Exploring What Makes a Book "Real"

When we reach that moment as teachers of "clearly we got this wrong," we have to reroute with the children. After all, this is *their* class. It is about their learning journey. It should center their questions. With this realization, I pondered: What were they thinking about publishing? How could this work become authentic and meaningful in the ways they were expecting? I knew that it was time for some more research as a large group.

During the children's working time (what some call "choice time"), I placed a variety of materials out on a big table. I included many of the children's different kinds of stories, pictures with invented spellings, handwritten teacher-scribed notes, stories written into their journals, and typed stories with children's illustrations. I also placed a wide range of different "published" works from the classroom and the school library. The children perused these different stories, getting ideas from one another's work, and carefully examining the "real books." They chatted informally, gathering information for our next discussion.

At our next meeting, I brought out several of the books from our collection and we sat down to look at them closely as a class. I asked the children:

- What makes a book "real"?
- How are our stories different from "real" books?

I asked these questions because I really wanted to get to the heart of the matter.

When I approached The Book Project, I wanted it to represent the real ideas and expectations that the children had about publishing. By asking these questions, I was hoping to get a better sense of what they deemed to be authentic and meaningful. They responded with a sense of calm confidence:

"Those library books are published, and ours isn't yet."

"The real books have a cover."

"Yeah, a shiny one. Real books are shiny."

"And a picture on the cover of the book."

"Books have a special paper that's shiny and has a smell."

"One of the books has pictures on all of the pages."

"It should have a name for the book. Books have names so you know what's inside."

"The pages need to go in the right order, like so that the right pictures go with the story."

"We need pictures of us because books need a picture of the author!"

"Yeah, those go on the back like a real book."

"It could have a reward [pointing to the Caldecott Medal award sticker], like this one."

"It needs to be in order, with numbers, so you can read it right."

As the children discussed, I gained a clearer sense both of their goals for The Book Project, as well as their understandings of books and how they function.

Dana knew that some "plans have failed because their authors designed them according to their own personal views of reality" (Freire, 2000, p. 94). She was keenly aware that she needed to act in accordance with the priorities and purposes identified by the children. And she wanted to ensure that the children's views, perspectives, and priorities were fully accounted for. But she wanted to ensure that their reflection was based on careful analysis—thus, her decision to invite them to inquire into materials that had been deemed to be published within the pre-K context.

TEACHERS AS LEARNERS, EMERGENT CURRICULUM AS MEETING EXPECTATIONS

To understand how this project unfolded, it is essential to understand two particular elements of the teaching and learning represented by this practice. The first is the teachers' focus on uncovering the specific elements structuring the children's concepts of what books are. The other element is the teachers' noticing, and noting of, the emergent ways in which the children are meeting so many of the expectations designated by our pre-K skills checklists. In fact, the kind of teaching in which Dana is engaging upholds high expectations for young children's literacy development *and* fosters critical consciousness—identifying dominant conceptualizations of authoring and troubling them together (Ladson-Billings, 1995).

As the project evolved within this space, Dana and Lucinda were listening carefully to these discussions, trying to fully understand the vision the children had and identify the necessary elements to make this project "real" to their students. Although this seems simple, it isn't. So often, we as teachers, as adults, miss the point even as we think that we are accomplishing exactly what the children desire. We fail to actually *ask* the children what they mean, what they value, what they see, and what they want, and to delve beyond face value, asking questions such as "Why?" and "Can you tell me more?" We need to ensure that children are not simply communicating to us what they think we want to hear. If we don't take such a step, we can easily end up being confused. This confusion is particularly dangerous in project-based work, when it always feels so child-centered . . . yet it may not be. Of course the kids want to build a cardboard fire engine. Of course they're happy writing less formal, unstructured "books." It sounds like so much fun that it seems like it is child-centered, but all too often we forget to ask. And in such moments, we impose our priorities and meanings, albeit well intentioned, and end up disempowering children.

As teachers, we are planners. We have been socialized into lesson planning, unit planning, project planning. Listening to children and following their lead does not mean that there isn't planning. In fact, there is an extensive amount of planning that goes into this process, as we envision what might be possible, integrate the skills that the children will need, and consider the paths that the project might take. We are always planning, shifting, envisioning, and scaffolding in order to make this work possible. Strangely, we often forget to ask the people for whom we are planning in the first place. The discussion above lucidly illustrates just how clear, how precise, the children are about their goals and their ideas. They know what this needs to look like, and their comments and questions offer a framework for goal-setting and organization for the whole project. We just have to remember to ask, to listen, and to position ourselves as critical learners who engage in reflecting upon these learnings and engaging in action within the context of our classrooms.

Some of the literacy goals addressed by the project were that the pre-K children would develop familiarity with different kinds of books, know how to handle books, display comfort with and care of books, be knowledgeable about the sequence and structure of books, and be engaged and interested in stories across genres. In addition to mastering these learning goals that were identified for us, there were many other literacy skills the children mastered. Thus, the teachers and students of Pre-K East went beyond externally identified learning goals. Yet, instead of a top-down approach, this happened in a meaningful and child-centered way. As you can see, the child-led investigation into the physical book, and the children's resulting comments, demonstrate so many of these skills, illustrating not just a sense of children who are authors, but children who have a nuanced understanding of the structure, function, organization, and aesthetic of the physical book. The children were also touching upon the mathematical concepts of number sense and sequencing as they considered the importance of page numbers in structuring a story.

All of these seemingly tiny details step forward with a sense of incredible vitality as they relate to the children's work and intentions, and they address learning goals in authentic and meaningful ways. The children do not care about page numbers because Dana told them to. They care about page numbers because they need them for the story they are writing. They are not noticing and noting the author page because Dana insisted that they notice and comment on it, but because they, too, are authors, and they need to know how to represent their authorship in a "real" way. As teachers create space for children's voices, questions, and processes, we bear witness to how these sometimes-disparate "skills" come together in an overwhelming chorus through emergent project work, as the children draw upon all these elements, upon their experience and knowledge, in pursuit of their own ideas.

Further, the children were interested in books and enjoyed reading them. They displayed print awareness, they were knowledgeable about books and displayed book-handling behaviors, they talked about books and stories and were starting to follow written words printed on the pages of books and to signify understandings and storylines in a variety of ways (through gestures, play, talk, and written symbols, such as letters). All in all, this inquiry process revealed the necessary elements that young children must understand as they develop early literacy (Clay, 2013; Owocki & Goodman, 2002), but more importantly, it made visible the elements of books that young children saw as essential and indicative of "real" or official books.

But . . . now that we had learned children's definitions of "real" books, how would the teachers honor the children's conceptualization of a published book? How would they communicate to the children that their work, that their stories, were worth publishing? In other words, now that they were aware, what would they do? How could they honor the children's definitions of "real books"?

"But How Can We Make Them Be Real?": The "Now What?"

In Pre-K East, teacher planning time is short and sparse. Lucinda and I have three meeting times per week; each is about 45 minutes, if we are lucky. By the time we grab some water and race to the bathroom, it's more like 35 minutes.

On this particular day, we sat across the table from each other in the glorious comfort of the 1st-grade-sized chairs, processing the day's conversation.

"So, they want a 'real' book," Lucinda said slowly.

"Yup," I replied, "glossy pages, page numbers, that new book smell . . . a 'real' book. How are we gonna manage this one?"

In this conversation, I could feel our teacher plans and expectations tugging loose, making space for the children, their goals, and their constructs of the real and not real. For a planner like me, it's a hard sensation, this letting-go of my carefully constructed paths to learning. It's also a feeling that I have learned to walk toward, knowing that we will accomplish more, delve deeper, if we allow our plans to become untethered, if we allow ourselves to ask about what might be possible. These are the times when I consider: What could be different?

"Well," Lucinda said with a smile. "We can just make a book. It's easy on Google Books." And she began showing me the formatting possibilities and book models we might use.

"How much money is left in the budget?" I wondered, and we looked, carefully tallying up the cost of the books, the number of copies we'd need to make, against the sum left in the year's budget.

"Do you think we could just print one for the classroom?" Lucinda wondered. "Then we could make something really big and beautiful."

"Nope," I said immediately. "We need to make one for every kid. It can be our gift to them, when they head up to kindergarten. See, I'm thinking that we would have a whole series of books that they take home at the end of the year."

"Yes, and let's try a lot of different kinds of bindings," Lucinda added, "because I know it's important to have a 'real' book, but I think it's even more important for them to have books that they know how to make independently. . . ."

Too soon, the hands on the clock pointed to 1:50 and we grabbed our stuff in piles, racing back down to our "resting" students, arrayed on their mats across the classroom floor. There is never enough time to talk, never enough time to plan, but these stolen moments at least give us a sense of where we might be going, a kind of lighthouse, generally leading us toward our destination. The creation of the "real" book would be a longer journey over the coming months as we worked on formatting and choosing which book would occupy this hallowed space. In the meantime, we took up more accessible forms of publication, hoping that the children would find validity in those as well.

CHAPTER 6

Science, Mathematics, and The Book Project

The Book of Paper Airplane Experts

"*Whoooooooosh!*" A large paper airplane soared over my head, across the unit block area, and then I heard "Hey!!" and "Ouch!" as it smacked right into Claire's head as she was trying to illustrate an extra-special part of her mermaid book at the writing table. The unexpected blow caused her to "make my line go the wrong way," thus ruining the drawing.

Trevor walked over, head down in dutiful apology, but also sneaking peeks at just how far this airplane creation had flown. It was really quite an excellent flight. Luckily, Claire is a reasonable child, and after Trevor helped her apply whiteout to the "ruined" part of the drawing, she happily went back to work. Before turning back to her illustrations, she looked at Trevor seriously.

"You messed up my work so you can't do that again, okay?" Trevor nodded, as he knew he should. "I'm really sorry," he said.

Then he turned to me, dismay on his face. "There's just not enough space!" he said, frustrated. "We're trying to make airplanes, and I didn't mean to bother her. I just wanted to see if it could make a long flight. So I could see if this was a supersonic!"

Now, I supposed that a "good" teacher might say, "No making paper airplanes in school." That seems like perhaps the definition of "good teacher" rules. But, true to form, I wondered aloud, "Well, where do you think you could go that would work? "

Trevor looked carefully around the classroom. I could see him mentally considering, and then dismissing different spaces: "Well, we tried Big Blocks, but the room is too round and small. We need, like, a long space for a long flight. Hey!" he exclaimed. "How about the cubby ramp?"

Our cubbies are arranged on a long ramp leading up to the lobby of the school building. It was the perfect space for airplane travel. It was also the perfect space to interrupt visitors to the building, our school administration, and our school nurse. "Okay," I sighed, "let's give it a try."

"Yes!" shouted Trevor, gathering his buddies and his supplies and heading out the classroom door.

This was the very beginning of *The Book of Paper Airplane Experts.*

In this interaction with Trevor, there are a few important things to be taken into consideration. Trevor had a plan. He was working with a group of children, Clay, Peter, and Alexander, who were all sharing ideas and testing out hypotheses. There was a high level of thinking and planning to their work, and so it deserved a space in the classroom. Unfortunately, as is often the case in our classrooms, the space was too tight for this kind of play and experimentation. But such tight spaces shouldn't hinder children's learning and development.

This conversation had important implications for the writing of a new book—a book whereby the otherwise discrete areas of literacy, science, and mathematics came together. Although, right now, as we are describing 4- and 5-year-olds making and flying paper airplanes it may seem like this interaction has little to do with book writing, the truth is, this discussion, these ideas, and the decisions that were made comprised the beginnings of a powerful authoring process for the children. This conversation also unveils the conceptions of science and scientific knowledge that young children bring with them to the pre-K classroom. It thus offers fertile grounds for science and mathematics teaching and learning. This is not an exception; it is a situated representation of how "science, technology, engineering, and mathematics (STEM) permeate every facet of our lives" (Berg & Mensah, 2014, p. 2).

SCIENCE AND MATHEMATICS IN PAPER AIRPLANE FLYING AND STORY AUTHORING

Recognizing airplane flying as story authoring, a site rife with potential spaces for scientific explorations and mathematical development, Dana and Lucinda supported the science learning of the young children in their class. They elicited students' ideas and planned for engagements with important science ideas, supported their thought processes, and invited them to develop evidence-based explanations. This process encompassed adaptations of the components of the framework proposed by Windschitl, Thompson, and Braaten (2018). As they worked, they continued to honor young children as curriculum codesigners, centering investigations on their questions. The paper airplanes allowed students to explore physics concepts in child-centered, authentic, concrete, and meaningful ways; to test hypotheses; and to record findings.

Since the National Research Council (1996) called for shifting the emphasis from enhancing students' knowledge of scientific concepts and facts to enhancing their ability to *do* science, it has been ever more important to build on the scientific experiences and inclinations children have, just as Dana did. Further, the *Next Generation Science Standards* (NGSS Lead States, 2013), which set forth standards, practices, and concepts to be explored from kindergarten onward, sought to develop a scientifically literate society, starting from the early years. What better time to explore scientific literacy than in the authenticity of play in pre-K?

"Doing science encompasses learning to question, observe, classify, communicate, measure, predict, infer, experiment, and construct models, as opposed to merely learning facts, concepts, and theories someone else has concluded" (Yoon & Onchwari, 2006, p. 419). Such a shift in focus means that teachers are no longer expected to impart scientific knowledge, but their roles have "shifted to involving children in doing science" (p. 419). Though this demands an understanding of the scientific concepts being explored, teachers are (re)positioned as facilitators of children's engagement in and with science.

In flying, estimating, and measuring airplanes and their flights (their size, weight, flight path and height), young children in the Pre-K East classroom made use of an extensive repertoire of mathematical concepts in their everyday lives (Ginsburg, Lee, & Boyd, 2008). In playing and experimenting, it is clear that young children, such as the ones in Pre-K East, "are capable of learning more and deeper mathematics than usually assumed" (p. 1). In fact, over 35 years or so, researchers have shown how young children develop "everyday mathematics—including informal ideas of more and less, taking away, shape, size, location, pattern and position—that is surprisingly broad, complex, and sometimes sophisticated" (p. 3). What Ginsburg and colleagues (2008) call "everyday mathematics" is developed in everyday situations, "usually without direct instruction" (p. 3). It develops simply because it "is so fundamental and pervasive a feature of the child's cognition that it is hard to see how children could function without it" (p. 3). This was certainly the case in Pre-K East.

Learning to See Children's Scientific Stories

The power and importance of The Book Project and similar projects, which empower children to author books and develop content-area literacy in subjects such as science and mathematics, rest in their ability to honor children's experiences, inquiries, questions, and priorities. They also rest on the interdisciplinary potential of such projects. Through The Book Project, areas of the curriculum such as science and mathematics are brought together with literacy in ways that are meaningful, authentic, and accessible to young children. After all, "mathematics education is (in part) education in language and literacy" (Ginsburg et al., 2008, p. 4). In fact, as Halliday (1993) underscored, language is the very foundation of learning.

Through these projects, we teachers are invited to see the children, their learning, and content areas such as science and mathematics with new eyes. We start to see in the stories that young children author and coauthor in the classroom, the mathematical and scientific knowledges and processes they encase. We become aware of how their stories interdisciplinarily braid multiple content areas (which often belong in different subject binders and are associated with distinct learning goals) in ways that center their questions. We urge teachers to see the potential for writing and authorship in these moments that can seem distant from traditional ideas of literacy. They are not! If we look closely—and most importantly, if we listen carefully—we can witness the beginnings of a story being authored. Yes, we have to be willing to let go of restrictive notions of authorship and conceptualize literacy and authorship much more broadly—in ways that are inclusive of young children's meaning-making processes.

How Can We Make Space for Airplane Play Inside a Pre-K Curriculum?

Based on traditional notions of learning and idealized portrayals of what classrooms should look like, there is an absolute desire to shut this kind of play down, to lead the children toward something more palatable, something that looks like more traditional "schoolwork." Yet this would be centering adults' needs and preferences and marginalizing children's meaning-making processes. Centering their interests and honoring their learning journeys, instead of shutting the paper airplane play down, Dana and Lucinda chose to sponsor the children's ideas (Brandt, 1998). They supported the children's thought and concept development as paper airplane play continued through the winter and spring months.

Recognizing that "written language encourages the development of metalinguistic awareness and children's monitoring and direction of their own learning processes" (Wells, 1994, p. 71), Dana proposed that the children turn this story into a book, so that others would learn from their experiments, from what they found. This happened within the context of the interaction below.

A "How-To" Book Emerges . . .

The work of the paper airplanes continued as new theories were offered, new constructions made, and new engineering plans tested. We watched videos of family members showing their own designs and tested different ideas. The "experts," who led the project, were getting overworked.

"Everyone wants us to make planes for them all the time!" complained Peter.

"Yeah, I can't even fly my planes because I'm always helping someone," added Alexander.

"It's getting to be a lot of work," Trevor sighed.

I couldn't help myself. I'm sorry, but sometimes that teacher-ness just jumps in and I cannot stop it. "Hmmm," I wondered, "is there a way that kids could know how to make the planes even if you weren't there or doing it?"

Trevor, wise Trevor with a 1st-grade sister, took the bait: "We can make a book!" he crowed. "It can be a 'how-to' book!"

Trevor, Clay, Peter, and Alexander looked closely at all of their work, the pictures we had taken and the words we had documented. They made choices, shared ideas, and thought about what was most important. When they were ready, they shared their initial ideas with the class.

As we looked at their work as a classroom community, we wondered how this book might be different than other books. The children offered the following ideas:

- This one shows you how to do something.
- You can make something with this book.
- It's real, like, you can really make something. Other books are just stories.
- The pictures are also different. This one has real pictures of people making planes. The other books have drawings.
- Sometimes books are about stories and characters and stuff. Sometimes they are about making things or how to do things.

The airplane experts sat at the front of the room, important in four chairs lined up, sharing their ideas and setting off inspiration throughout the classroom. As they shared their draft and ideas, the class noted what worked in their book and offered comments. The authors developed new ideas and identified edits they would like to make.

The Book of Paper Airplane Experts emerged from the children's long-term investigation into the dynamics, physics, and capabilities of paper airplanes, melding physical and mathematical concepts, and resulting from many scraps of paper where children had written recordings of time, distance, speed, and weight, considering each of these variables in relation to one another. It was a how-to book using images of children, their concepts, their drawings, their mathematical measurements, and their tracking of paper airplane flights. This book illustrated the integration of mathematic and scientific concepts into the language arts work of young children. It documented the use of design thinking, mathematical concepts, spatial relations, and measurement through the children's investigation into paper airplanes. As a part of The Book Project, the children gathered the information developed through airplane experimentation and, as one of the children explained, "made it into a book so other kids will know what to do. Like, how to measure how far or how to make a supersonic and stuff."

THE INVESTIGATION: READING AND WRITING TOWARD ACQUIRING INFORMATION

The Book of Paper Airplane Experts captured an investigation into the physics of flying in a child-centered and child-authored manner. It contained children's measurements (of time, speed, and distance) descriptively and comparatively. It was framed as a "how-to" book, which meant that it had an orientation toward acquiring new information, whereby readers are learning something new that they will take away after the reading (Rosenblatt, 1978). That is, the children had hoped that readers would seek to build and fly paper airplanes after reading their book. It was not a book predicated on in-the-moment reading enjoyment, but one that taught skills to be applied afterward. In making such a decision in the authoring of this book, the children in the Pre-K East class had communicated their understanding that authors and readers approach books from different perspectives.

The work of this book was framed around the children's questions and the experiments they used in order to answer these questions (see Figures 6.1, 6.2, and 6.3 for examples of pages from the book). With each new piece of information they discovered, came new questions. These questions were carefully recorded as a way of documenting their process. Dana worked with the paper airplane experts to integrate their questions into morning meetings, using the morning message as a site to share them, so that everyone could offer ideas and share their hypotheses—regardless of whether or not they were directly involved in the experiment.

Some initial questions the children had were:

- Why do small planes fly straighter than big planes?
- Is it the throw or the weight that makes it go fast?
- Which one goes farther, a big plane or a small one?
- Can planes fly inside when there's no wind?
- How can we tell how far it went?
- How can we find out how much farther the other one went?

These questions offered a framework for the experiments the children conducted as they developed this project and its accompanying book. And some of them ended up being addressed in the book (see Figure 6.4 for two examples).

In response to the last two questions about distance, the class decided they needed a tool to track distance. They began by making a large chart (which can be seen in Figure 6.3), much like the one used to chart the weather each day in their pre-K classroom. "That way, we can write down how far it went!" announced Peter. This chart led to a few more questions: How do

Figure 6.1. *The Book of Paper Airplane Experts*, Science Investigation

Science Investigation:

Airplanes

Many of us have been working on paper airplanes over the past few days, and we are asking interesting questions about why and how paper airplanes work. Today Clay, Trevor, Frank, Stephan, Simon, and Alexander worked with these materials, asking questions and testing out hypotheses.

Questions:

- Why do small planes fly straighter than big planes?
- Is it the throw or the weight that makes it go fast?
- Which one goes farther, a big plane or a small one?
- Can planes fly inside when there's no wind?
- How can we tell how far it went?
- How can we find out how much farther the other one went?

We explored these questions during working time. We experimented with different:

- shapes,
- paper weights, and
- techniques of throwing the planes.

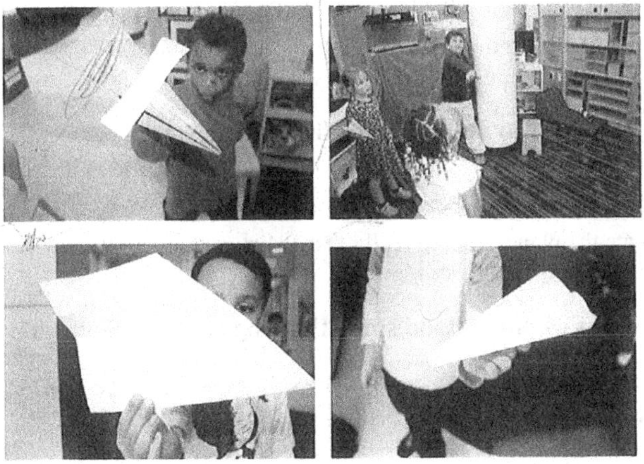

Figure 6.2. *The Book of Paper Airplane Experts,* Theories and Questions

We tried to answer our questions and found we had developed some theories and many new questions.

Why would small planes fly straighter than big planes?

- Maybe it's about the weight? Maybe the big ones you can't throw as fast?
- The big one feels heavy
- The small one is fragile but it goes really fast.
- The little one flies straighter. I think the big one has too much weight so it turns

How do we know the flight path of the plane?

- Maybe it's the throw or the weight
- The wings make it fly, so it's probably the wings

What about the air and the wind?

Air is really strong

- It flies better outside because there's no things to crash into outside
- It could get swept away in the wind outside
- On the real plane there's stuff on the bottom and stuff behind and paper airplanes don't have it so it can't fly very long

They spin really fast to make a plane fly

- So the wings, the air is under the wings. The wings are so flat that the air is under it and the air pushes it up
- I notice the plane is going really fast. That gets in the jets and the faster the airplane goes, the higher it gets

A drawing helps us understand some thinking about airflow and lift

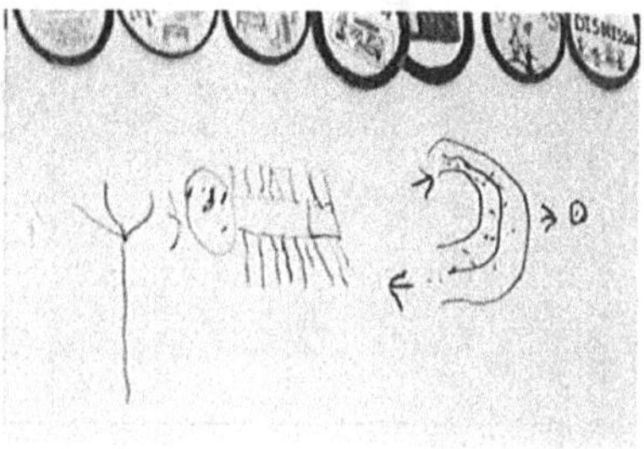

Figure 6.3. ***The Book of Paper Airplane Experts,* Questions**

Questions:

How can we tell which planes go the farthest?

- We can measure it like how far the first plane went and then how far it went?

What does "measure" mean?

- Measure is to find the size like with numbers
- You can measure how far something went, but I was trying to tell how far from the other planes
- We can put tape on the floor with our names. Then we can know where the planes went and we can measure them

Making Our Chart and Documenting Our Flights

How will we measure when the flight is longer than our measuring tape?

Figure 6.4. Some Questions Included in the Book

How do I teach someone else to make a plane?

How does a different shape make the plane fly?

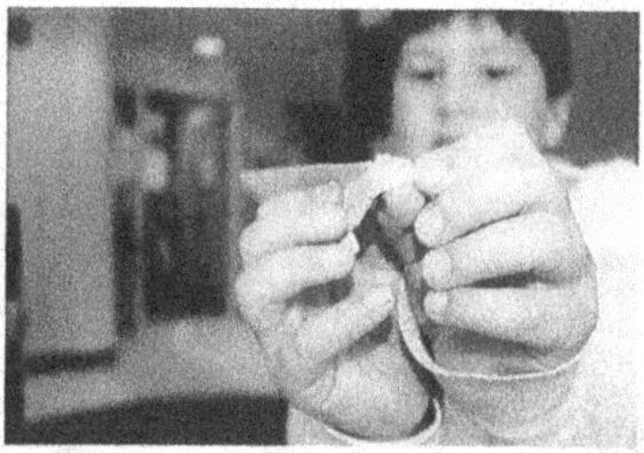

you know how far something went? How can you tell? What does "measure" mean? Here are some of their answers and subsequent questions:

- Measure is to find the size like with numbers
- You can measure how far something went, but I was trying to tell how far from the other planes
- How will we measure when the flight is longer than our measuring tape?
- We can put tape on the floor with our names. Then we can know where the planes went and we can measure them

After testing many different tools, including rulers, yardsticks, and tape measures, the class decided that measuring with their feet was the best method, "Because then everyone can do it and we all need the same kind of measurer so our numbers measure the same thing for the races. That's fair, see?" explained Trevor. With the airplane ramp set up outside our classroom, the chart in place, and an agreed-upon method of measurement, children began tracking their experiments. Though they would eventually find out the trouble of measuring with their feet (different-sized feet, the need to engage in addition and modified multiplication—with, of course, the aid of manipulatives), they were on their way to writing a new kind of book that featured their newly developed scientific expertise.

FROM EXPERIMENTING WITH PAPER AIRPLANES TO AUTHORING "HOW-TO" BOOKS

As they continued their discussion of how-to books, it became clear how, through children's questions and their ensuing discussion, a new door had opened to authorship in the classroom. Expanding the universe of authoring by considering the authoring of how-to books, one student, Emory, wondered: "Does the book have just one kind of plane, or lots of planes?" The classroom community thought about Emory's question. The children soon began to expand the possibilities available to them:

- We could make more books for other planes.
- We could actually make books about lots of things.
- Yeah, like how to do things. Then people will know how to do lots of stuff.
- Does it have to be about planes?
- No, we know how to do more things than planes. It's just the making part, and showing how to do it.

How-to books became part of formal and informal authorship work in Dana's pre-K classroom. This was apparent in the last comment: "We know how to do more things than planes. It's just the making part, and showing how to do it." Suddenly this was a whole new space for authorship and writing. In addition to stories, the children could share what they knew how to do. They were exploring genres in and through authoring in meaningful and authentic ways, in ways that prioritized their questions and honored their voices. Book genres were identified not because some adult had decided, but because their coauthored books served different purposes, and some of these purposes were better served by particular genres.

It is important to note that this work emerged in the early spring, when the children had developed a stronger sense of themselves and their abilities in the classroom. They also had developed as members of a learning community. They were beginning to think of the next year, of who they would become and what they might leave behind. This very traditional construct of the how-to book became a space for self, a space for ability, expression, and confidence in what they knew and what they could share.

The work of the how-to book also allowed children to engage in metacognitive work themselves. Whereas Dana had modeled such a process before (as explained in Chapter 5), now they were engaging in thinking carefully about their own thinking. They asked questions such as these:

- How did we make the airplane?
- How did we do a braid?
- How did we construct a Magna-Tile®[1] building?

These were essential questions for how-to books. The process had to be made visible—the whats, the hows, and the whys. The children in Pre-K East also had to think empathically about their audience, carefully considering how someone might follow their directions and what information that person might need to know, to be told, and to be shown. The writing space was reconceptualized by the pre-K children as they engaged in authoring how-to books. It became a collective space. It became a space where children developed and tested hypotheses, recording the outcomes of their experiments. In this space, markers and pencils touched papers while at the same time hair was braided and paper airplanes were folded and flown. In this space, the children sought one another out to read their descriptions and offer peer feedback. As the children came together in this space, they saw one another as experts. They regarded one another as individuals who could and would teach their classroom community something—through the authoring of a how-to book. As such, this once-traditional writing space was turned into a space of meaning, possibility, and self—a space of authorship.

It had been *The Book of Paper Airplane Experts* that opened up this possibility in the Pre-K East classroom, making space for a new kind of authorship. But it had also been Dana and Lucinda, as teachers, who made space for paper airplanes to fly within the structure of their pre-K class, and who had sponsored the children's literacies. In doing so, Dana and Lucinda had sanctioned authorship together with the children within and across the content areas, bringing together science, mathematics, language and literacy. Together, they developed as authors, as scientists, and as mathematicians. And they also developed their scientific and mathematical literacies.

---

1. Magna-Tiles® are magnetic tiles for building three-dimensional structures. For more information, visit www.magnatiles.com.

The writing of *The Book of Paper Airplane Experts* was long and complex, as the authors worked to share their ideas, edit their work, and make certain that nothing was left out. They constantly asked questions, offered and tested hypotheses, recorded their findings, and shared their learnings. Here are some of their initial questions and hypotheses, which catapulted into science experiments and resulted in lots of mathematical records, comprising evidence:

Why would small planes fly straighter than big planes?

- Maybe it's about the weight? Maybe the big ones you can't throw as fast?
- The big one feels heavy
- This small one is fragile but it goes really fast.
- The little one flies straighter. I think the big one has too much weight so it turns

How do we know the flight path of the plane?

- Maybe it's the throw or the weight
- The wings make it fly, so it's probably the wings

What about the air and the wind?

Air is really strong
- It flies better outside because there's no things to crash into outside
- It could get swept away in the wind outside
- On the real plane, there's stuff on the bottom and stuff behind and paper airplanes don't have it so it can't fly very long

They spin really fast to make a plane fly
- So the wings, the air is under the wings. The wings are so flat that the air is under it and the air pushes it up.

As they sought to answer their questions with evidence, the children took on the role of scientists and mathematicians. They explored important ideas in science—ideas that went far beyond the scope of the learning goals set forth for pre-K. As they developed evidence-based explanations and answers to their questions (regarding the flight path of planes and the role of wings and wind direction and speed in determining flight paths), findings were added to the book. Through this process, the children and teachers sought outside resources to expand their knowledge, consulting books, sharing experiences, exploring new spaces (indoor and outdoor), and speaking with experts to deepen their work. In particular, they were joined via Skype by a parent who was particularly adept at making paper airplanes. He demonstrated his skills to the class, and explained his ideas as to why certain paper airplanes went faster than others. The children were engaging in reading, writing, science, and mathematics, not as a mandate or as top-down academic pressure, but because their questions demanded answers, which could only be authentically answered through interdisciplinary methods . . . in pre-K.

And when their book was ready to share, share they did. They had been talking about their work and about their findings in the classroom, at home, and on the playground. So it was no surprise that others were excited to learn from these pre-K students' learning journey through *The Book of Paper Airplane Experts.*

Sharing *The Book of Paper Airplane Experts*

One morning, when the work was finally done, there was a crowd around the art table. A group of children from the other pre-K class had joined us and they were all peering at something. When I approached the table, I saw *The Book of Paper Airplane Experts*. Children were looking at the pages, carefully pointing at the images and making folds in their papers.

They were talking:

"No, look, you do it like this."

"See, Peter folded it like this!"

Different planes were emerging as they thumbed through this new book. The paper airplane experts were not really relieved of their duties. Far from escaping the work, they were drawn to the excitement their work had created, helping out, explaining their ideas, and jumping in when "you're doing it wrong!"

The book was well used by the end of the day, and we had to print more copies of it. This book was a new tool, and we were making good use of it.

One could say that the book was a success. It authentically served its purpose. It taught others how to make paper airplanes—not only any paper airplanes, but the paper airplanes that would reach the longest distances over the shortest time. The children who were reading the book paid careful attention to the kind of paper used (some weighed more than others), to the size of the paper (because the size of the plane mattered), and the folds and angles, keenly attentive to the details and directions which would result in the construction of the fastest possible paper plane. And the experts, age 4 and 5, helped; after all, they had plenty of experience and tons of evidence . . . just as scientists do!

CHAPTER 7

Observation, Language, Poetry, and The Book Project

One of the intriguing things about this work is that sometimes as a teacher you just have to follow it, carefully recording children's words, documenting their journeys, without—at the time—fully understanding the life it will take later on in the school year. Then, at some point in time, the small moments you documented and the conversations you recorded emerge as something important and meaningful for that particular community of learners. This requires a great deal of trust. That is, you have to trust that the children's journeys, their words, and their interests will become important threads in the fabric of the learning that will unfold in the classroom. You have to do so without the sense of immediacy that often permeates commercially available curriculum guides. You have to respect young children's timelines—to trust that at some point in time, they will tell you.

It is within this trusting, child-guided timeline that, all of a sudden, the children may indicate that they are ready to revisit something that took place days, weeks, or months earlier. Although, in our experience, we have found that we may forget the details and intricacies of what happened, the children often don't. That is why it is important, as teachers, to document, to record, to capture children's journeys, so that we can join them in their next learning adventure.

Careful and thorough documentation is crucial for an emergent curriculum to develop. It serves as an important archive of the history of a classroom, of how a learning community grew. And history matters. It is as we follow the words of the children, document the changes in the classroom, and write its history that new possibilities are born. And so it was in the case of how the children in the Pre-K East classroom engaged in poetry and authored a multipart poem about how seasons change: "All of the Seasons Square, a Season World."

"The Shape of the Words Is Different"—All of the Seasons Square: A Season World

"All of the Seasons Square, a Season World" was a poem that began to be authored before we knew it was a poem. It was not something that was intended. It was something that became through the life of our classroom, just as the children and we adults are in the process of becoming all the time.

It was a late September morning—September 23, to be exact. I know because I used the date as a way of labeling the children's writing that day. It was one of those incredible New England days in the fall, when the children are still wearing shorts and T-shirts, but there is that tiny bite in the air when you wake up in the morning. The green leafiness of the summer has just a whisper of red and orange at the tips, and the promise of apple-picking trips and Halloween costumes is all around us.

Part of our work as teachers of young children is to help them to notice, to observe the world around them, to name it, to describe, and to make meaning through this process. Too often, the world is presented to children as something that just happens, something of which they should somehow have an implicit understanding, despite the fact that their memories and their meanings are still in the making. And so, as teachers, we need to teach them to pause. We need to make time for them to consider, to describe, to notice, and to come to understand themselves as a part of this world, their world.

As a passionate lover of fall, I was ready to do some noticing of the changes in the outside world, unveiling how seasons work through firsthand observation. I wanted to mark these changes with the children, to hear their language develop as they came to understand how what was unfolding in front of our eyes was a regular repeating pattern of change in weather, which led leaves to change color. I wanted them to recognize that the daylight was being temporarily shortened and then elongated for us (while at the same time being temporarily elongated and then shortened in the Southern Hemisphere), all a result of the Earth's rotational axis tilt and the Earth's orbit further distancing us from the sun.

As we marked the changes in the outside world together, as a teacher, I marked the changes in the children who entered the classroom weeks ago, unsure and often tentative. That feeling began to recede in the precarious confidence born of late September. We were deep into honeymoon season, where the children come into the classroom with a wobbly sense of bravado, enough to fuel their excitement, but still tempered by newness. Late September is a lovely time in the story of a class.

And so, on this day, we sat in a circle outside on the playground and called our meeting to order. This was a different thing, this meeting outside, but the children's newness called them to attention, all of them wanting to prove that they knew the rules, were certain of their job, despite the different environment. Such are the gifts of late September.

As we sat, I asked the children to look around them. "What do you see?" We paused to wonder. Then I asked: "What do you notice? Is everything the same, or are things changing?"

The children looked around them, quickly at first and then with more purpose. "What is it like outside today? Do you notice anything about the season?"

After a brief period of quiet, Claire carefully raised her hand and said: "Not fall yet but soon."

The class was again silent for a moment, turning Claire's words around in their heads, and then looking to me.

"Great words, Claire," I said. "I'm going to write them down so that we can save them. You said, 'Not fall yet but soon.' Is that right?" She nodded shyly. More hands were raised. On that day, I collected these words:

- Still a little summer
- A little bit fall and a little bit summer
- Half fall and half summer
- Some days it's fall, some days it's winter

When all of the raised hands had been acknowledged, I asked a new question: "Today we will do some very small paintings using just the colors you can see outside today. These paintings will stay at the back of the classroom, on the board, and we will send them home at the end of the year. What do you notice? What colors do we need to put out to do this painting?"

This question was easier, and brought forth comments from some of the more reticent students. They explained:

- We need brown; that's for the trees and the bark.
- And brown for some of the leaves. Just a few.
- We need lots of green! There's still lots of green.
- And just a little bit of red and orange.
- And a tiny bit of yellow!
- I actually think we need pink.
- Trees aren't pink!
- Oh yes, look at the edge of that leaf!

They all looked and noticed the delicate pink edging on a leaf that was beginning its fall change. They were right. I guess we always need a bit of pink.

Armed with the children's observations and their color ideas, I trooped back into the classroom, setting up the large table with paint based on the children's color choices.

The work we began that day, early in the school year, would be the first step in a yearlong study of the outside world, which centered our observations and our descriptions of that space.

ON THE IMPORTANCE OF CIRCLES

The Pre-K East culture circle meetings always took place within the physical context of a circle. Although this may seem obvious, we want to unveil the importance of circles for learning. In the circles, the very physical arrangement serves to break hierarchies that are too often present in traditional classrooms. Circles counter the positioning of the teacher as the holder of knowledge. Circles are "space[s] in which all views can be voiced freely and safely. Only when all views are heard can we claim that the heterogeneous nature of our culture is most widely represented in the circle" (Bahruth & Steiner, 2000, p. 123).

The seating arrangement in circles stands in opposition to the traditional banking concept of education, in which knowledge is deposited in students' brains as money into banks, as discussed in the Introduction (Freire, 1970). In circles, teachers do not stand in front of the classroom; they sit with and alongside the students. Students, instead of facing their teachers, from whom they are to learn, face one another, in acknowledgment of one another's expertise (Souto-Manning, 2010). Thus, the physical seating arrangement in circles is essential to employ dialogue and engage in problem-posing education (Bahruth & Steiner, 2000; Freire & Macedo, 1995). This is because this "circular seating is conducive to dialogue. It allows students to look at each other, see everyone, and value everyone's voices" (Souto-Manning, 2010, pp. 34–35).

It was within the physical context of a circle and within the pedagogical framework of culture circles that Dana and her students engaged in this seemingly simple discussion. As they observed, named, and questioned changes and uncertainties in the world around them, they were in the process of integrating several different skills and concepts related to children's literacies, scientific thinking, observation, and artistic practice. They were also engaging in the process of reading the world, problematizing it, and engaging in a dialogue in which they all felt heard and included. Although this process pertained initially to the physical world (the sink overflowing, leaves changing), eventually it would include children's observations and readings of their social and cultural worlds. Making the culture circle framework concrete at first was key for the development of a process that would guide learning within this learning community—as it came to explore more abstract concepts later on.

CHILDREN'S OBSERVATIONS: READING THE WORLD

The first step in reading the world (Freire & Macedo, 1987) with young children is to dedicate time for observation, for a close reading of their physical world in all its concreteness, then inviting them to share their noticings, their readings, and honoring their observations as an act of reading. In doing so, we can communicate to them that their world can be read, and engage them in doing so.

In our experience, it is rare in their fast-paced lives filled with school and other scheduled activities (often to accommodate their parents' and other family members' busy work schedules and demands) that young children are afforded the time to really look, experience, and respond to the outside world. Despite our constant lack of recognition (noted by its absence in curriculum guides and learning goals), reading the world plays an important role in children's literacy development in particular and learning in general. And so, Dana makes space for this kind of observation in her classroom, venturing outdoors and encouraging the children she teaches to describe and express what they notice about the world around them—to read the world.

Through reading the world and sharing their observations, the children can come to guide the work of the classroom. For example, as Dana and Lucinda took their pre-K students outside to observe the changing leaves and notice the dropping temperatures, among other things, they were positioning the children as producers of knowledge. As they met in a culture circle, the children discussed the colors they noticed. This allowed comments to be made, questions to be asked, and disagreements about colors to emerge. This is a simple yet critical way in which the children are framed as "in charge" of and responsible for their own learning and for their own classroom. They quite literally see the classroom changing in response to their observations and the decisions made through their discussions. The curricular offerings in the classroom were determined by those observations.

Through this process, the teachers explored an integrated approach to observation of the outside world, the seasons, changing colors, and language and literacy knowledge that grew over the course of the year. Instead of serving as the authority who determined who was right, Dana asked questions such as "What do you think?" and "What evidence do you have?" She positioned herself as a facilitator. Yet, in effect, she introduced complexities to their dialogue, problematizing their noticings. She often took on the role of *difficultator* (a concept coined by Augusto Boal, 1995). As the difficultator, Dana generated participation (ensuring that multiple voices were heard and valued) and recognized the complexity of critical learning processes. She stimulated her students, culture circle participants, to ask questions that problematized (overly) simplistic or reductionist readings of the world (Cahnmann-Taylor & Souto-Manning, 2010).

As seasons changed, children closely observed and recorded those changes. They shared their documented observations and used descriptive words and phrases to depict what they saw. Then they did a painting to capture and re-present their observations. These responses (written and painted) were hung on the classroom wall and grew over the course of the year. The children read and reread their words, ultimately creating a poem and large-scale artwork that integrated their descriptive language, scientific observations, and creative imagery portrayals of the outside world. After all, "poetry . . . has the advantage of covering any and every subject one can think of, literally and figuratively. Nothing is out of bounds for it" (Brady, 2009, p. xiii).

As the year went on, the children's process of observation and description in and through art became part of the classroom routine. With routine, children's confidence and comfort in the practice developed. Certain of their own understanding of the shape of this work, children began to push themselves. They started to make connections and to play with the routine, adding complexities and difficultating it.

All of the Seasons Square: A Season World—January 8

In early January, as we were headed inside, pulling off snow boots and wringing out damp mittens, Frank pulled on my arm.

"Dana," he said with some urgency, "it's really different outside now."

"Yes," I replied, too intent on tugging off Claire's snow boots to pay much attention. "It's definitely different." I grunted, tumbling backward as the boot finally came free.

"But that means we need to do the thing!" he continued, now pulling my arm in an effort to help me get upright again. I was currently on the floor, mixed up in the jumble of boots, snow pants, coats, and other outdoor gear that take over our cubby area in the winter.

"What thing?" I asked, detaching an errant Velcro glove from my backside.

"You know, the thing! Where we write about the outside! The colors are totally different now."

Realization finally dawned on me. He was completely right. Our world of reds, oranges, yellows, and browns had given way to the cold whites, blues, and grays of winter. The large back bulletin board in our classroom had stopped in the fieriness of late fall (Figure 7.1). It was time to write and paint again.

"You're right!" I agreed. "Let's do that tomorrow morning for meeting."

Frank smiled with relief that I was finally on board. Teachers can be so dense sometimes.

On the following day, we sat in a circle as a class. We began by rereading the words we had written in prior months. Before beginning to share new ideas, we wondered: "How are our words getting different? Are they the same from the beginning of the year?"

This was not a time of silence. The kids noticed right away the evolution of their work and wanted to share with the group:

- In the beginning it was so short but then it was longer and longer.
- That's because we know more stuff.
- Yeah, we're older and we have more words in our heads.
- We need more words for kindergarten!

With these ideas about their shifting words at the forefront of our thoughts, we moved forward with our description of January 8:

- Frozen season
- More frozen than a frog frozen inside of ice
- The winterest day of the year
- Frozen river
- Wintery
- The winterest day
- Snow fall, snow ice
- No rainbows, ice freezing
- Snowy but no snowflakes
- Ice season
- Freeze
- Snowy Outside
- So icy
- The sprinkle day
- Slippery season
- The ice, snow, sparkle day

POETRY AS A LANGUAGE ART: MAKING MEANING AND MAKING SENSE THROUGH ART

We regard authoring as a key element of inquiries. And by authoring "in different ways, we discover new aspects of our topic and our relationship to it" (Richardson, 2000, p. 923). Poetry has particular affordances for inquiry, as it is "a method of representing and of making meaning" (Greene,

Ellis, & Simecek, 2016, p. 357). And so, in the Pre-K East class, the children explored their changing environment through poetry—making meaning of and representing their experiences. The "poetic function of language" met the pre-K children's "deeply human need to symbolize" (Simecek & Ellis, 2017, p. 112).

As a language art, poetry holds an important place in teaching and learning processes; "poetry is a way of constructing lines and meanings in spoken or written work" (Brady, 2009, p. xiv). This language art and graphic art-making process with the children was truly powerful because of its constant presence in the pre-K classroom. Yet it was a seemingly simple practice. With each discussion, Dana set out the colors chosen by the children with a small set of watercolor notecards, liquid watercolor paints, and brushes. When completed, each small painting was added to the back board of the classroom, creating a large, collective expanse of colors and representations from their observations of that season. The teachers also added the words the children had composed that day, hanging them beneath the series of small paintings. The resulting work, which brought words and images together, was stationed at the large back bulletin board in the room (see Figures 7.1 and 7.2 for examples of their display in the classroom). It was a visual reminder—both physical and mental—of the changes they had experienced as a part of the class.

As illustrated in the above portion of the story that unfolded in Pre-K East, the children were able, in a concrete way, to see their own evolution in terms of the language they employed and the descriptions they offered. They engaged with the "aesthetic features that would define language" (Lindfors, 2008, p. 1). They noticed that their words were getting longer and more complex. This served as inspiration for the development of more descriptive language and a deeper connection to the world around them. Their poem clarified the communicative purpose and the necessary intentionality of authoring. That is, authoring should be about something; it should do something . . . even if this something is aesthetic.

As evidenced in the comment "We need more words for kindergarten!" the children saw their growing vocabulary as part of their growing selves. As we referred back to their older writing, they remembered their younger selves and those earlier days of school. In doing so, they inspired themselves, but also raised the level of their work as they moved toward the inevitable heights of kindergarten. This was not a quest to amass words or to address what Hart and Risley (2003) have called the "word gap." This was a child-centered and child-owned growth process, a process whereby they noticed their vocabulary developing and their words carrying meaning, communicating their particular noticings.

So often, writing work with children is about artifice, some writing prompt, theme, or expectation of what writing or a book might be. And unfortunately, many times young children come to internalize this. They write stories about princesses, astronauts, and superheroes. This is not to say that we want to eradicate those fanciful characters from young children's authorial forays and writing repertoires—far from it. But we also want them to know that authoring is also deeply linked to who we are, to who they are. Through authoring, we can engage in describing our world and in bringing ourselves into being. Through authoring, we situate, but we also become situated. Through authoring, we become. Through these words, these descriptions, and their evolution, the child says: "Here I am. I am here. Here is how I see my world, and myself inside of that world. And I have the tools to make that meaning, through my words."

All of the Seasons Square: A Season World—May 16

Real spring in New England is nothing short of miraculous. This is because of our certainty that it is never actually coming. While other parts of the country traipse through the daffodils in late March, we are often still digging our cars out of snowbanks. Those April showers are typically icy cold, soggy, and incessant in Cambridge, Massachusetts. It is a time of mud, cold, wet, and waiting. Then, finally, spring arrives. The skies clear, and those flowers that have been waiting in the cold and mud finally burst forth.

As a class, we take to the outdoors immediately, peeling off our layers and racing around in shorts and T-shirts in the balmy, 50-degree weather. It's miraculous.

It's also a time for a new addition to our writing and painting. After an extended romp of outdoor play, we returned to our circle, ready to document on the board the words of this new world that had emerged outside.

"Okay, what should we write down?" I asked, dry-erase marker poised:

- Leafy green
- Bumble bees making honey
- Feels like it's warm on your skin
- You can have lemonade at this time
- You need a cold drink
- Foggy summer
- Spring—it's pretty and flowers and vegetables are growing
- Rainbow shave ice
- No snow pants allowed
- No coats
- Ice cream
- Trees are growing big
- Flowers are growing tall

- I like how the air smells
- Sunny
- I feel like I want a beach
- Olaf melted
- Becoming more beautiful. . . .

Those last words ended on a sigh, and Clay said, "Hey, can you read it all together? Like, all of the words from the beginning?"

"Sure," I replied, and we turned to look at our paintings at the back of the room as I pulled down all the words to read in order. I read through our September selves, our October fire, the frigid feelings of our January and February, and finally our ecstatic May (see Figures 7.1 and 7.2).

When I finished, we sat, thoughtful, as realization dawned on us:

- It's a poem!
- Yeah, it's a poem because of how the words go together.
- We're all the authors because it's all of our words.
- It gets longer at the end because we have more words.
- It's a poem because I can see things when you read it, like, things in my head.

We wondered, "What makes it a poem? How is it different from our other stories?" The children pondered the writing, the shape of this new creation, and began to offer their observations:

- It's shorter.
- The shape of the words is different.
- It's more like, about things like seeing things, and not like something happens like in a story.
- It doesn't have ninjas.
- It just sounds like a poem. Like, when you read it, it sounds like a poem happening and not a story with people and stuff.

It is amazing to me that a poem can just happen. I would like to be able to tell you that it was my intention all along to write a class poem. I had many other good intentions about language, description, vocabulary, and observation, but I did not see the poem until the children saw it. But then there was something so powerful about the discovery of our poem, and the children's naming of their work as poetry. And it was *their* discovery, *their* naming.

Writing a Poem . . . and What Is a Poem?

Through this process, their careful consideration of words, of what words can do, of how their words changed, and how words shape their thinking, they arrived at a concept of a poem. There is nary a rhyming word in this poem. Many of the vestiges of traditional children's poems are absent, and yet the children could hear the poetry in the shape of the words, the imagery that was evoked, and the way "the words go together." Defining "poetry according to pre-existing forms . . . does not measure the uses to which poetry can be put as methods of representation about life" (Brady, 2009, p. xiv). In this sense, the pre-K children's poetry was about "sharing meanings about being human that in turn can lead to social action, in and out of the classroom" (p. xiv). It was an artful assemblage of their words, of their phrases, of their language.

Together, the children's words "spoke against academics' habit of setting up poetry as esoteric, its creation and interpretation reserved for an exclusive few in the society" (Sloan, 2001, p. 47). The teachers and the Pre-K East class had claimed poetry, "knocking it off its pedestal, bringing it down to earth within reach for all" (Sloan, 2001, p. 47). Within the context of the Pre-K East class, "playfulness, not pretension, was the essence . . . of poetry for children" and by children (Sloan, 2001, p. 47). This is a democratic view of poetry. This is the view the pre-K children embraced.

This collective meaning-making, both in the making of the poem and of what it means to be a poem, was deeply personal for the Pre-K East classroom community. It was not about a teacher saying, "And now we will read a poem, class. A poem is. . . ." After all, there is "no process of analysis by which a poem can be taken apart to show why it is poetry or why it is not. It is something intensely felt or it is nothing" (Smith, 1953, p. 111). As verbal art, poetry in the Pre-K East class was about everyday life. Yet it allowed the children to see their everyday experiences and the world in new ways. Within the context of this class, poetry became a powerful art form—a verbal art. While not being able to predict the future, Dana and Lucinda had a sense that the children would carry with them these ideas of poetry as they read and write in the years to come.

When the children decided on a title for their work, they did so as they do all things: in a big circle. This time, the big circle took place in the familiarity of the purple rug. Many ideas were bandied about and words written on the board. Finally, after much debate and word shopping, the pre-K community assembled a name that everyone could agree upon. It was a name that reflected the story told by the poems, as well as the images of all the children's paintings, a sweeping swath of colors swinging from fall, to deep winter, and finally to spring and their graduation to a new world: *All of the Seasons Square: A Season World.*

Figure 7.1. *All of the Seasons Square: A Season World*, Part 1

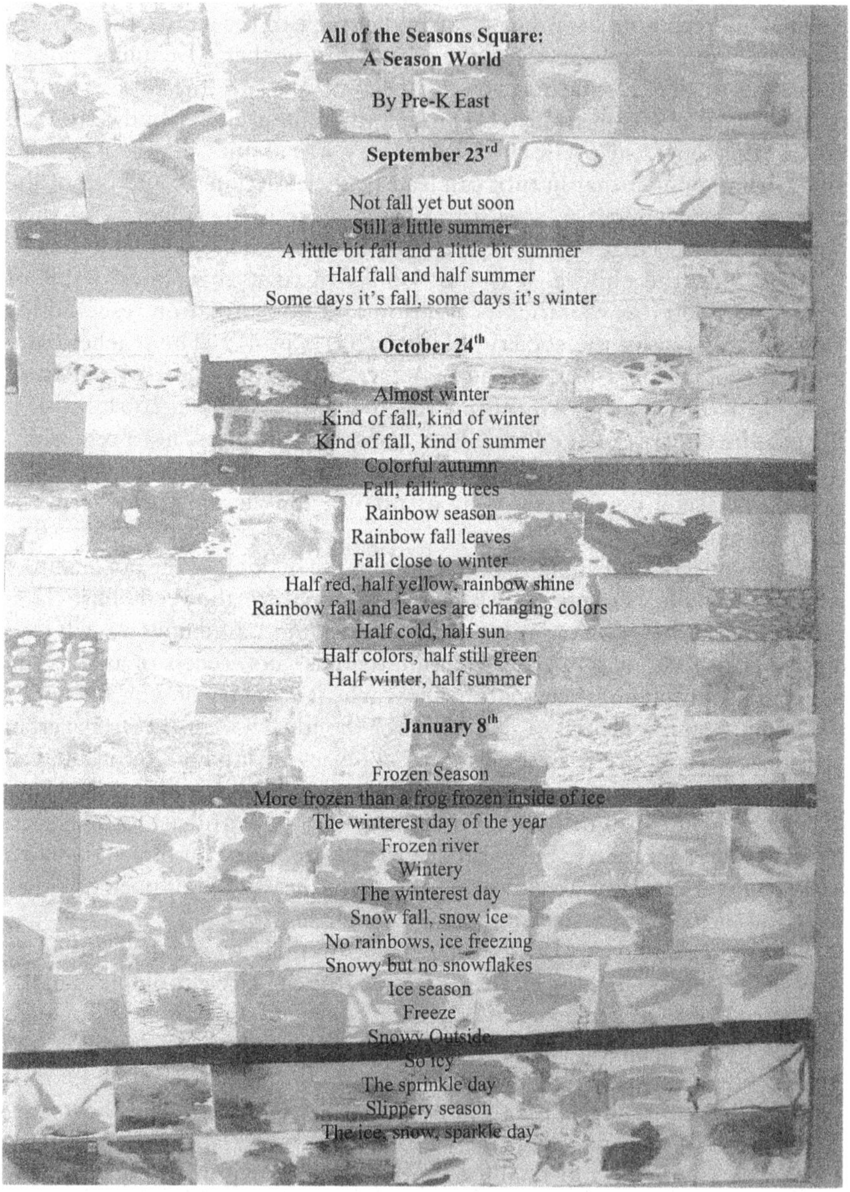

All of the Seasons Square:
A Season World

By Pre-K East

September 23rd

Not fall yet but soon
Still a little summer
A little bit fall and a little bit summer
Half fall and half summer
Some days it's fall, some days it's winter

October 24th

Almost winter
Kind of fall, kind of winter
Kind of fall, kind of summer
Colorful autumn
Fall, falling trees
Rainbow season
Rainbow fall leaves
Fall close to winter
Half red, half yellow, rainbow shine
Rainbow fall and leaves are changing colors
Half cold, half sun
Half colors, half still green
Half winter, half summer

January 8th

Frozen Season
More frozen than a frog frozen inside of ice
The winterest day of the year
Frozen river
Wintery
The winterest day
Snow fall, snow ice
No rainbows, ice freezing
Snowy but no snowflakes
Ice season
Freeze
Snowy Outside
So icy
The sprinkle day
Slippery season
The ice, snow, sparkle day

September 23rd

Not fall yet but soon
Still a little summer
A little bit fall and a little bit summer
Half fall and half summer
Some days it's fall, some days it's winter

October 24th

Almost winter
Kind of fall, kind of winter
Kind of fall, kind of summer
Colorful autumn
Fall, falling trees
Rainbow season
Rainbow fall leaves
Fall close to winter
Half red, half yellow, rainbow shine
Rainbow fall leaves are changing colors
Half cold, half sun
Half colors, half still green
Half winter, half summer

January 8th

Frozen Season
More frozen than a frog frozen inside of ice
The winterest day of the year
Frozen river
Wintery
The winterest day
Snow fall, snow ice
No rainbows, ice freezing
Snowy but no snowflakes
Ice season
Freeze
Snowy Outside
So icy
The sprinkle day
Slippery season
The ice, snow, sparkle day

Figure 7.2. *All of the Seasons Square: A Season World*, Part 2

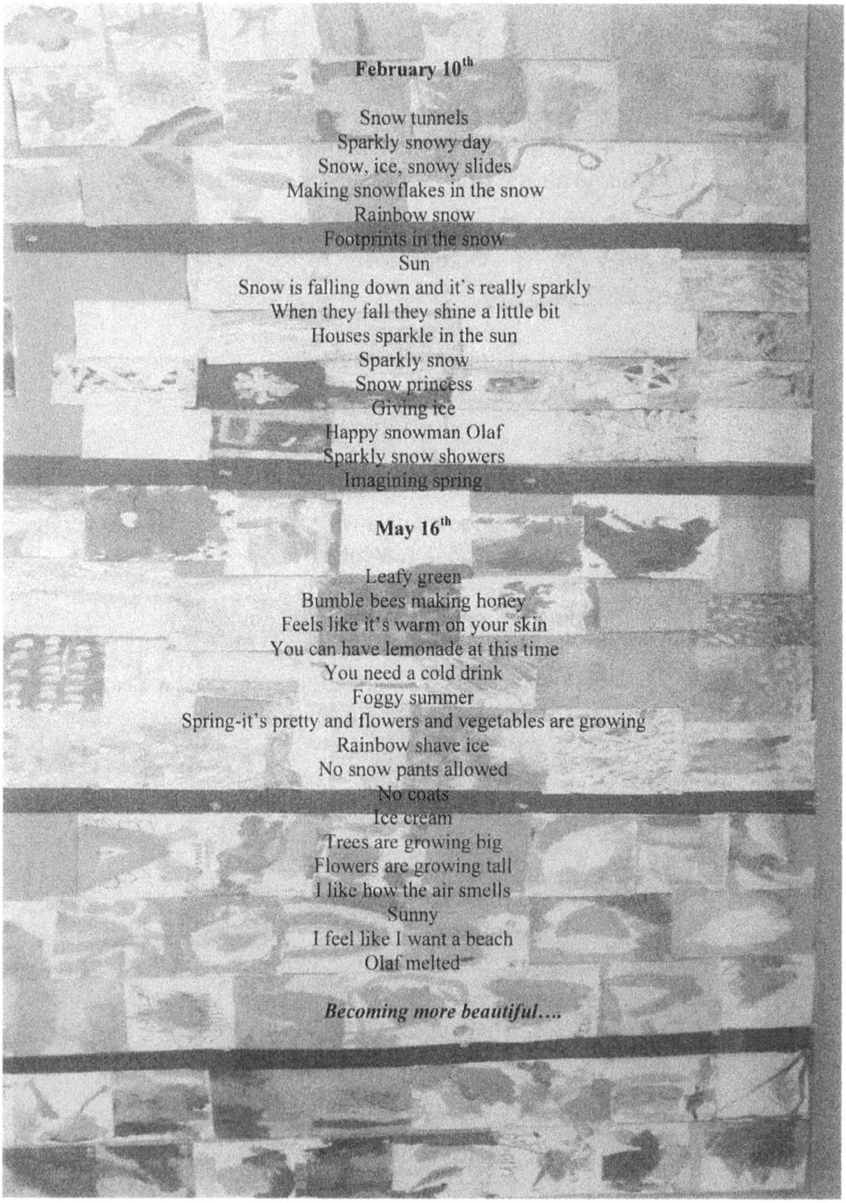

February 10th

Snow tunnels
Sparkly snowy day
Snow, ice, snowy slides
Making snowflakes in the snow
Rainbow snow
Footprints in the snow
Sun
Snow is falling down and it's really sparkly
When they fall they shine a little bit
Houses sparkle in the sun
Sparkly snow
Snow princess
Giving ice
Happy snowman Olaf
Sparkly snow showers
Imagining spring

May 16th

Leafy green
Bumble bees making honey
Feels like it's warm on your skin
You can have lemonade at this time
You need a cold drink
Foggy summer
Spring-it's pretty and flowers and vegetables are growing
Rainbow shave ice
No snow pants allowed
No coats
Ice cream
Trees are growing big
Flowers are growing tall
I like how the air smells
Sunny
I feel like I want a beach
Olaf melted

Becoming more beautiful . . . .

REFLECTING ON CHILDREN'S LANGUAGE AND LITERACY DEVELOPMENT IN AND THROUGH POETRY

As can be seen in the children's processes and products, their language and literacy developed in the process—and so did they, as learners. They honed their observation and documentation skills as they recorded their observations with rich descriptions, which used figurative language, engaging with poetry as verbal art (Britton, 2003). They employed figures of speech in order to make their poetry more persuasive and impactful, engaging with poetic language while also "drawing attention (through sound, syntax, and patterns of meaning)" to the symbolic nature of poetry (Simecek & Ellis, 2017, p. 112). The figures of speech they employed allowed them to engage in playing with words—not by making nonsensical words, as is often the case in prescribed curricula for pre-K. Instead, their word play afforded them the use of words, which went beyond their literal meanings in sophisticated and knowledgeable ways.

A common feature in poetry, figurative language is often used as a literary device. The pre-K children used figurative language for emphasis and to signal resemblance (such as the reference to Olaf, the snowman character from Disney's *Frozen*). They delved into the use of similes, making comparisons that established similarities (for instance, *More frozen than a frog frozen inside of ice*). They made allusions to adult language, using expressions that had been employed to regulate their dress (such as *No snow pants allowed; No coats*). They employed imagery, using figurative language to represent ideas in ways that may appeal to the reader's physical senses (*Feels like it's warm on your skin*). Through symbolism, they communicated ideas (for example, the phrase *Bumble bees making honey* communicates it's no longer winter; it is springtime) and employed alliteration (*Bumble bees*).

As the pre-K children explored and expanded their use of language, engaging with figurative language, they developed their vocabularies in meaningful and authentic ways. They carefully considered words and phrases, talked about their meanings and relationships, and then chose the best words and phrases as they authored their poems. Beyond figurative language, these pre-K students' understandings and authoring communicated that they saw the "use-value of poetry . . . that is tied to the aesthetics of such texts" (Simecek & Ellis, 2017, p. 98).

The students considered the aesthetic nature of poems—how readers might experience the reading, how they might feel "during the actual reading event" (Rosenblatt, 1978, p. 24). Yet they understood that "poetry is something that is active, reflective, and open-ended" (Simecek & Ellis, 2017, p. 108) and acknowledged how readers are likely to respond to and engage with their poetry differently. For them, poetry was more than the use of poetic features. The pre-K children recognized their poem as "a cultural artifact of a symbolic kind . . . used to mediate the individual perceiver-subject's activity in the social world" (p. 107).

In addition to developing their vocabularies, the children in the Pre-K East class added a new genre to their repertoire as authors. They had authored stories, how-to books, and poems. They explored genres, voices, and audiences. They were not merely consuming vocabulary, but analyzing and engaging with it in ways that deepened their understandings of how language works. In doing so, they developed a strong sense of themselves as capable and accomplished authors and came to understand the unique affordances of poetry. And although it was not a book, the children's collectively authored work of verbal and visual art, *All of the Seasons Square: A Season World*, became part of The Book Project.

As a teacher, Dana knew that the "educational value of poetry—its utility in formal educational settings such as schools—is lost when it becomes a tool of a testing regime or a deliverer of transferable skills because of a lack of attention to the aesthetic experience the text gives rise to" (Simecek & Ellis, 2017, p. 99). Thus, she purposefully resisted any urge to tame children's poetic explorations or to constrain their poetry authorings. She did so because she knew that, like philosophy, poetry offers the potential to "catch us in the act of being. What could be more fundamental to knowing the human condition than that?" (Brady, 2009, p. xvi). And the poetry her students authored did just that.

CHAPTER 8

Social Studies and The Book Project

Social studies work occupies so much time in the work of the early childhood classroom. It is always there as children make decisions regarding the life of the classroom community and consider the injustices in the larger society in which they live. Social studies can foster civic competence and engagement, helping young children develop an understanding and respect of civil and human rights. But how exactly does it come to life in the early childhood classroom? "As children learn to get along, make friends, and participate in decision making, they are engaging in social studies learning" (Epstein, 2014, p. 78).

Not only does social studies help children understand their role and responsibilities as citizens in a diverse community, it also helps them understand the interdependent world in which they live. In the early childhood classroom, social studies aims to foster the development of young children who can prioritize the public good via well-considered and reasonable decisionmaking processes. After all, early childhood classes are some of the first communities of which young children become part, outside of their kinship communities. Within the context of early childhood classrooms, young children explore community roles, negotiate rules, seek to create and participate in a democratic society (or a community, which serves as a microcosm of society), and develop understandings of concepts from disciplines such as ecology, economics, history, and geography (Epstein, 2014).

HOW SOCIAL STUDIES COMES TO LIFE IN THE PRE-K CLASSROOM

For the children in the Pre-K East classroom, social studies is about themselves, the families to which they belong, and the communities of which they are members. It is also about society and the wider world—especially how they can come to understand and position themselves in relation to that wider world. The pre-K students considered the following questions as they sought to understand their social worlds and their very locations within them:

- Where are we in the world?
- What is our history?
- How should we be in the world?
- How do we want the world to know us?
- What might we do to shape the world?

These were the enduring questions that shaped the work of 4- and 5-year-olds, questions that evolved in shape and depth over the course of the school year, making space for new possibilities and offering new challenges. Thus, naturally, these social studies pursuits wove their way into The Book Project, nudging their way into the culture circles in the class and asserting themselves into the pre-K project work.

But before we consider how, here we briefly pause to consider: What *is* social studies? We offer the definition authored by the National Council for the Social Studies (NCSS, 2018):

> Social studies is the integrated study of the social sciences and humanities to promote civic competence. Within the school program, social studies provides coordinated, systematic study drawing upon such disciplines as anthropology, archaeology, economics, geography, history, law, philosophy, political science, psychology, religion, and sociology, as well as appropriate content from the humanities, mathematics, and natural sciences. The primary purpose of social studies is to help young people develop the ability to make informed and reasoned decisions for the public good as citizens of a culturally diverse, democratic society in an interdependent world.

Although we may initially think that this definition excludes young children or may be too abstract to come to life within the context of a pre-K class, young children are very committed to issues of fairness (Paley, 2007). Fairness "in relation to political decisions is especially central in a democracy" (Verba, 2006, p. 499). Thus, fairness and democracy "are expected to go together" (p. 501). Specifically within the early childhood context, when young children solve problems together in the classroom and seek to determine what is fair and right together (as illustrated in this book), they are engaging in a situated representation of the democratic process (Gartrell, 2012).

Social studies comes to life in pre-K in rather concrete ways (Seefeldt, Castle, & Falconer, 2010). After all, according to NCSS (2010), "the aim of social studies is the promotion of civic competence—the knowledge, intellectual processes, and democratic dispositions required of students to be active and engaged participants in public life" (p. 1). As Epstein (2014) explains, though learning standards for social studies in early childhood vary by state, they address some common themes: "(1) membership in a democratic classroom community, (2) location and place relationships, (3) similarities and differences in personal and family characteristics, (4) basic economic principles as they relate to children's lives, and (5) appreciation of one's own and other cultures in a diverse society" (pp. 78–79).

In the following two class-authored books, entitled *A Book of Family Shares: A Book That's Happy with Our Family with Our Family Pictures* (henceforth *A Book of Family Shares*) and *The Pre-K East Life Book*[1], you will see the children addressing several social studies questions, including these:

- What is the story of my family? How can our story become part of our work at school?
- What is the story of my/our life in the pre-K classroom? How can I keep that story even after I am gone?

The pre-K children explored what Epstein (2014) explained as the two components of social studies in early childhood education: social systems and social concepts. "Social systems are the norms, values, and procedures that affect human relationships in our day-to-day lives" (p. 79). Social systems include the roles that people play (in homes, communities, and larger society) and democratic processes. It invariably entails experiencing diversities in perspectives, points of view, identities, and cultural norms. The second component, social concepts, includes economics, history, and geography. In learning about their own families and documenting their development as a learning community, the children in the Pre-K East class dabble into social systems and social concepts in child-centered, meaningful, and authentic ways. This happens as they engage in authoring the books identified below.

In *A Book of Family Shares*, the children in Pre-K East engage in an exploration of their own histories, from the day that they were born, taking an anthropological perspective, coming to understand themselves as historical beings and relating their own timelines to the timelines of historical events (Souto-Manning & Martell, 2016). Then, in *The Pre-K East Life Book*, the children documented their own community, its rules, and more, delving into the development of their classroom community as a social system and writing about how they developed as citizens of a learning community. In

1. Though their titles are similar, *The Pre-K East Life Book* and *The Whole Pre-K East Book* are distinct books. *The Pre-K East Life Book* was the text that the teachers were attempting to make into a "real" book using online publication resources. The beginnings of this work were referenced in Chapter 5.

doing so, because (as you may remember) they wanted a "real book," they engaged with economics and geography, social concepts, wrestling with the costs of printing a "real book," considering where it was coming from, and where it would be published. We now turn to the process of authoring and publishing the two books, part of The Book Project.

A Book of Family Shares: Discovering "When-I-Was-Little"

It was early morning in the Pre-K East classroom. Susan walked hand-in-hand with her daddy, confidently making her way through the sign-in routine and the morning message. Our message asked a question about memories. Upon reading it, Susan immediately became animated.

"Daddy!" she cried, tugging on his arm, "tell me the story that you remember."

Her dad looked at her, bemused. "Which story, sweetie?"

"The one of when I was a baby! You know it!"

Her dad looked at her again. "There are so many stories of when you were a baby. Which one do you mean?"

Susan threw her hands up, exasperated. "The one when I rolled over and got stuck on my tummy. You know!" she exclaimed, almost affronted at the idea that there might be any other stories of significance.

"Oh, that one!" her dad responded with relief, and launched into the retelling of what was clearly a much-loved childhood story.

"Tell it so Dana can hear it," Susan insisted, and her daddy raised his voice a bit to share the memory.

As I listened, I reflected on the story, and the incredible delight that Susan took in its telling. It was not a long story, nor was it dramatic, but these moments of "when-I-was-little" carried so much glamour and warmth.

When he was done, Susan sighed. "I love that story," she said, smiling with contentment, "and now Dana knows it, too!"

I had a feeling in that moment, just a sense that there was something more here, something to be made of this quiet moment between father and daughter. Later, during morning meeting, I asked Susan to share the story with the class, which she did with pleasure.

". . . And then I was just stuck on my tummy and I got so mad that my face was bright red!" she finished with aplomb. Her when-I-was-little story sparked the interest of the class, and so many children had stories that we decided to go around the circle to do a group share. When they were done, Susan contemplatively raised her hand.

"That was fun," she said, "but it's better when my daddy tells it. He remembers all of the little parts."

"Yeah," agreed Margo. "I like to hear how my mommy tells the story better than me."

As we talked, it was generally agreed that we liked to be told these stories, rather than being the tellers.

"Hey!" said Alexander, always ready with an idea. "Maybe we can invite them to come and tell the stories at school!"

"Yes, and write them down, too," added Simon, always thinking.

"It could be a book of when-we-were-little," added Susan, not to be left out of the inspiration.

And thus, a new book began in the pre-K classroom: a book of home, of family, and of memory—a book about the history of the individuals who made up our classroom community.

FAMILIES AT THE HEART OF THE SOCIAL STUDIES CURRICULUM

This tiny moment of Susan and her father telling stories in the early morning of the Pre-K East classroom became a powerful component of the social studies work in The Book Project. When this moment was lifted up to the rest of the class during our morning meeting, it was clear that these family stories held power and interest for the children. One unique element of this process of storytelling was that, for the first time, the children did not want to tell the stories themselves. As demonstrated by their conversation, they found their own retellings of these stories to be inadequate. They needed their families and caregivers to do the telling, regarding their stories as family funds of knowledge, "historically accumulated and culturally developed bodies of knowledge" (Moll, Amanti, Neff, & Gonzalez, 1992, p. 133). Their families not only knew their stories, but could also make connections to their own stories and the stories of those who came before them. They could offer details regarding cultural practices and social relations across time and space. As a result, those stories were much richer.

The children's comments clearly indicated that families were capable storytellers; they knew their stories and their histories. These stories were not *yet* written down or published in books, but they could be . . . if the pre-K class just undertook a research study, documenting the histories of their very beginnings from the perspectives of their family members (Souto-Manning & Martell, 2016). This was important, the class determined, as they recognized that they all had histories and they were all stories worth telling (Lester, 2005). And this is how the children in the Pre-K East class started engaging in primary source research, learning from the stories told by family members and carefully analyzing associated artifacts (pictures, documents, and so forth).

The element of "when-I-was-little" was something that they clearly wished to bring into the classroom, to connect with their identity within the school. These were stories that the children wanted told as they started understanding themselves as historical beings (Freire, 1970; Souto-Manning

& Martell, 2016). They also had the potential to afford anthropological insights, as pre-K students engaged in the study of humankind along with its culture, society, and environment, as represented in their classroom community through their collective stories.

Engaging Families

The children's initiation of what would become *A Book of Family Shares* offered a rich opportunity to invite families into the classroom in an authentic way, integrating them meaningfully into a classroom project and offering a connection between home and school life and between humankind in general and humankind as represented in the Pre-K East class. This offered the potential for the children to engage in what could be termed *anthropology*, a situated "study of human beings and their ancestors through time and space and in relation to physical character, environmental and social relations, and culture" (Anthropology, n.d.).

Yet sometimes these family invitations can be intimidating. Family members often have many questions about what to bring, how to prepare, and what the expectations are. And this was no exception. As the families asked these questions within this setting, the answers were simple and left them feeling reassured. Dana answered their questions by saying:

- Tell us a story about your child/children that tells us about who they are.
- If you want, share some photos or photo albums.
- And . . . ask your children.

As an official invitation, the pre-K students wrote a letter to their families. The letter was sent home on a two-sided sheet of paper. On one side, it had the children's original writing and illustration (see Figure 8.1). On the other side, it had the following typed message, transcribed by Dana as the children read their letter aloud:

Dear Families,
Please come and tell a story about your life. We want to put it in a book. Then we can send the books to our families. We can make copies so everyone can have one. The stories could be about:

Snee boarding
Skiing
Disney World
Weddings
Cooking
Being scared

Birthdays
Florida
Costa Rica
And
Summer and Spring

You could also tell another story. We love you.
Love,
Pre-K East

As Dana explained: "This is because sometimes grown-ups forget how to read children's writing, so we have to help them a bit."

Over the course of several months, each family was invited into the classroom to share stories of their children. As a community, they shared baby pictures, apple-picking techniques, grocery-shopping adventures, adoption stories, and fears of lobsters. The family stories were very alive and real, each carrying powerful components of that child's history and identity into the body of the classroom. As a teacher, as Dana reflected, the most striking element of this experience was the sheer individuality of the shares.

Dana was initially afraid that this would take on a repetitive sameness, as though the children have internalized a protocol of the acceptability of certain stories, resulting in a litany of "my family vacation" stories, one decipherable from the other only because of the faces in the snapshot. Or she feared that it would take on a competitive imprint, as families raced to showcase the most impressive experience; however, as families came in, it was clear that while the pre-K children were members of a learning community, they were also powerfully unique individuals who belonged to other communities within an ever-interconnected world.

Somehow this process resonated with its uniqueness. Children showed pride in the simple elements that constituted their family cultural practices and that informed identities, from how they spend a particularly good Saturday morning to their favorite drawings from preschool. As each story was told, the texture of the fabric of "us" shifted and expanded, including new elements of the children's identities in our collective understandings of one another.

On Listening and Being Heard

When undertaking projects such as this, there is always the question of how the children will respond to one another. This question can paralyze teachers and halt possibilities for learning. After all, it is such a delicate balance. As a teacher, Dana knew that one snide comment, one dismissal during the

Figure 8.1. Letter to Families

Dear Families,
Please come and tell a story about your life. We want to put it in a book. Then we can send the books to our families. We can make copies so everyone can have one. The stories could be about:
Snee boarding
Skiing
Disney World
Weddings
Cooking
Being scared
Birthdays
Florida
Costa Rica
And
Summer and Spring
You could also tell another story. We love you.
Love,
Pre-K East

first share would compromise or shut down the process forever, inspiring fear and self-consciousness in the children and denying the vulnerabilities necessary in telling their real stories.

This project occurred in the spring, after the children had had many months to develop a respectful community and an understanding of the culture circles framework that structured class discussions. Dana was thrilled to find that it was with these skills that the pre-K children entered into this family-share process, eagerly clamoring to see baby pictures, gasping in excitement over snowy mishaps, thoughtfully questioning birth and adoption stories, and demonstrating a genuine enthusiasm that inspired candidness and vulnerability in all of the storytellers.

With each new story, it was as though students were discovering new rooms in a house that they thought they knew, wandering around and coming to know one another more fully. The memories of these shares emerged again and again over the rest of the year. As these stories were invoked and memories shared, as a community, the Pre-K East students engaged in deepening and further connecting the circle between their home and school selves. In a situated way, this helped the pre-K children develop a better understanding of the workings of multiple interrelated social systems.

Through this process, the members of the Pre-K East community learned about the histories of each member of the classroom community. They came to understand "The History of Us," which was initially "an oral language project" (Souto-Manning & Martell, 2016, p. 62) and later was turned into a book. The book would become part of The Book Project.

Taking Charge of the Text

It was mid-May when I finally heaved a sigh of relief, crossing the last family off the family-share scheduling list. Though this process brought great richness to our classroom, the scheduling and organizing were a burden. I suppose good things often are. It was then that I began the process of transcribing the stories, meeting with each student and checking my notes and retellings of their memories. It wouldn't do to get it wrong.

"No, no!" exclaimed Susan, our original story collector. "It's reach, twist, and then pull. That's how you get the apple and don't damage the branch!" I quickly edited the page, reflecting her revisions.

After the stories were revised, I printed a copy of the book for each of the children. Several of us were gathered at the large back table in the room, reading our stories, making comments, and mostly looking at the family photos accompanying the stories crafted from our shares. I thought this was the conclusion of our project. It was published, right?

As Simon rifled through the pages, he propped his head in his hands. I watched his thinker pose with pleasure and trepidation. It almost always signaled a new idea, but usually one that would demand a massive overhaul of the original plan. Without warning, he slapped the table with a start.

"You know what, Dana?" he said, his voice a strident staccato. We all raised our heads, unstartled, but listening. We were used to Simon's antics at this point in the year, but also well aware of his work as an idea person.

"We need pictures," he explained.

"Well, we have pictures, see? I've printed out the pictures of everyone's families."

"No, no," he said, waving his hands, frustrated. "Like illustrations. These are just pictures of the storytellers. We need to draw illustrations for our stories. That's how real books go. You know that. It's not just a picture of the author."

Heads around the table were beginning to nod, and I sighed in surrender. I had already printed copies of the book for every child in the class. I had organized them neatly, and this element of our project was now about to be laid to rest. Instead, I consigned these pages to our drawing paper pile, and turned my attention back to Simon, who was now excitedly collecting the drawing pencils to begin illustrations.

It was true. Books do have illustrations. And the stories would be more powerful for the children if they took control of creating imagery for their work. And thus, *A Book of Family Shares: A Book That's Happy with Our Family with Our Family Pictures* was revised once again, a reflection of the children's vision of themselves and their families in the body of the classroom.

The children in the Pre-K East class knew what the parts of books were. They knew who they were as authors. And they saw themselves capably. This is what allowed Simon to trouble how finished or ready the book Dana had printed really was. The book was revised to include their stories, the storytellers' photos, and the children's illustrations. Examples of these three components can be seen in Figures 8.2 and Figure 8.3, which present pages from *A Book of Family Shares*.

AUTHORING OUR HISTORY AS A COMMUNITY

We now ask you to return to *The Pre-K East Life Book*, giving continuation to the story we started in Chapter 5. We do so as a way to signal that these two projects coexisted. They were not self-contained, but were threads within the fabric of the pre-K curriculum. And they offered fertile grounds for the integration of curriculum. Although *The Pre-K East Life Book* was initially explored within language arts, now, we unveil how it is also a social studies project.

The Pre-K East Life Book was a book written in the spring. It represented the shared memories of the learning community in the Pre-K East class. After initial "publications" of other texts, the children came to problematize the meaning of "publishing" and had requested the creation of a "real book" as a part of their project. After all, a bunch of pages filled with symbols and stapled together did not, in the children's perspective, comprise a real book. It did not look like or smell like a book. While the teachers continued with other forms of publication over the course of the project, they

Figure 8.2. Stephan's Family Memories: Story, Photo, and Illustration

Stephan's Family Memories

Stephan's family memories were filled with wonderful experiences with his big brother and sister, Kristof and Kailin. During his share, we learned that Stephan loves to dress up. Some memorable costumes were: a cyclist (like his dad), Spiderman, an astronaut, and characters from Ninjago. We learned that Stephan is always kind and polite, but also very determined. Our favorite family memory happened during a family skiing trip when everyone was trying out some ski jumps. Stephan and Kailin skied down and fell on a jump. They were soon followed by Kristof, who said "Wheee! Whee! Whoooaaa!" as he fell down too! By the end of the story, the whole family was tumbled together in the snow, laughing.

Figure 8.3. Dominique's Family Memories: Story, Photo, and Illustration

Dominique's Family Memories

Dominique and her family shared many funny and cute baby memories of Dominique. We learned that Dominique was a mischievous baby who loved to find special places to hide, and sometimes got stuck! Our favorite photo pictured one-year-old Dominique hiding in a cabinet. She is a wonderful helper, and we saw many photos of Dominique helping around the house by sweeping, washing dishes, and (trying) to fold the laundry. We also learned that Dominique sometimes goes into her auntie's closet and dresses up in scarves and high heels! We also got to meet Dominique's very first stuffed animal, who was given to her when she was a tiny baby in the hospital. Some of Dominique's favorite things are: going to the beach, swimming, getting dressed up, eating, and cuddling.

were also researching the creation of a "real" book and looking for the title that would occupy this important space. *The Pre-K East Life Book* became the subject of this all-important publishing endeavor.

The Pre-K East Life Book

It was an early spring morning in the Pre-K East classroom, a thoughtful sort of morning. The day before, we all visited the kindergarten classrooms for a short time. The children met the teachers and checked out the spaces that would be theirs next year. The mood had been one of wild excitement and enthusiasm for kindergarten. Today, however, a quiet set in. We were, as always, sitting in a circle on the rug. A small blond head leaned on my shoulder and a soft brown hand rested on my knee. It was a time to be close.

"Do you remember the time when we held the baby chicks? Those ones that were in the egg and got born?" Dominique mused.

"Oh, yeah!" exclaimed Simon. "I was afraid it was gonna poop on me!"

The class giggled, and I wondered what path this conversation would take.

"Do you remember the time that we played monster tag and Claire was the monster?" asked Marcus, warming to the theme.

The "do you remembers?" flew across the circle, and I could feel the children coming together through shared stories, building on remembrances, and strengthening themselves in unity as they faced the uncertainty of kindergarten.

There are moments to step in as a teacher and take the reins, and other moments when you let their voices and ideas wash over you like a waterfall, awaiting the path they will take when the water finally finds its destination. And so it was with this conversation.

"Hey," said Simon, his body jerking excitedly as it does when he has an irrepressible idea. "We should have a life book."

The class was silent, unsure of his meaning.

"Yeah, a Pre-K East life book. Then people can know about us when we are in kindergarten. They can know the things that we did, and how to do them and stuff."

Awareness dawned on the rest of the class as heads began to nod. "Then they will know our 'do you remember' stuff!" Clay exclaimed, blessing the idea with his approval.

"Yes, and it's *The Pre-K East Life Book*, because that's our life at school!"

"The life of our community."

Ripples of excitement crossed the circle as the children began to conceptualize this new book, what would be our last book. The unease of the earlier morning seemed to have settled. There was safety in the knowledge of being remembered, of our "do you remembers" being saved in a *Life Book*, which could never be forgotten.

The pre-K children knew that it was important to document their history as a community. This would allow them to be remembered. After all, there is a seeming fleetingness to these early years in school, a sense of constant forward motion juxtaposed with the endless routine and familiarity of the classroom day. The children thrive in these spaces, gaining confidence through their understandings of one another, the knowing and being known in the classroom. Yet, as the end of the school year drew ever nearer, they knew that change was coming. It was that change that met their needs and allowed space for their growth.

But it is often challenging to find a home for young children's fears, for their natural unease as they face these massive changes. With these changes, seemingly ahistorical beginnings are sanctioned. They wonder: How do I know I will be remembered? I have lived a lifetime in this room. How will others know what that lifetime was? And as they enter new classrooms with new teachers, the children's negotiations and history as a community are often silenced, seemingly forgotten. And as new children enter the classroom space (physical and relational) that once was theirs, these new children are often unaware of its history and legacy.

The book Simon proposed could serve both purposes: to inform future pre-K students and to educate their future teachers about their learning history in pre-K. That is, the creation of *The Pre-K East Life Book* spoke to the social needs of the class, their individual needs to be known, and the collective need to demonstrate the "we" (Dyson & Genishi, 1994) that they had become through their shared stories, adventures, and lives that wove themselves together over the course of the year. It also served as a historical and anthropological account of their life in pre-K. As the final book in The Book Project series, *The Pre-K East Life Book* was a motley collection of the history of the community, of how and what they wished to be remembered, and of the lives that they wanted to freeze in time for their memories and the memory of others.

What Is a Memory?

To begin the project, they needed to make certain that they were all working with some shared understandings or commonly understood vocabulary. Using the official space of the morning message, Dana asked the children the question "What is a memory?" to prepare them to discuss these ideas as a group. As they met for another culture circle to trouble common understandings of memories, whose memories matter, whose memories have historically mattered and why, the children offered the following:

- A memory is something that you know about from a long time ago. You might forget, but you remember.
- Memory is like when you remember something.
- A memory is like where if you did something awesome and you always remember it.
- It means you remember what you did a long, long time ago.
- It's just when you remember something.

As Dana listened to the children, she realized that the stories they had been sharing were part of the memories of the pre-K classroom, and so did they:

"Maybe we should put those words in the *Life Book*," suggested Susan, "so people will know it was a memory. Because we know what it is. 'Cause we were there, playing monster tag and stuff. But they weren't there."

The children agreed to put some of their words about what a memory is at the beginning of *The Pre-K East Life Book*, offering guidance to readers (see Figure 8.4). It was important to help the readers who weren't there and might not know what the pre-K class meant by memories, how they made sense of their life in pre-K retrospectively. After all, the book captured the pre-K class's social memory, developed within the context of the classroom community. This is important because "it is in society that people normally acquire their memories. It is also in society that they recall, recognize, and localize their memories" (Halbwachs, 1992, p. 38). And because *The Pre-K East Life Book* sought to capture and convey their social memories, retrospectively authoring their history as a community, it had to be "a really real book."

"A Really Real Book"

As I discussed the making of this book, I wanted to make certain that I understood the children's visual understanding of what the book might be. After making several books in the classroom, visits to the 1st-grade publishing party, and our trip to the bookbinder[2], we had many ideas on how books were made. When the possibilities were discussed in the meeting, Marion raised her hand: "The *Life Book* should be a really real book!"

"What do you mean?" I asked, bemused. Heads were nodding around her, but I was left unsure. "How does a book become 'really real'?"

"It has a hard cover," said Frank.

"Oh yes," agreed Marion, clearly grateful for the backup, "and the pages are . . . you know . . ."

"They're kind of shiny!" exclaimed Susan.

"Yes, shiny!" Marion agreed, "and they have the real book smell."

Simon nodded his head vigorously. "And it has all of that little writing in the beginning, you know? With words and numbers?"

"We didn't make a book like that before," said Ella, "and that's what real authors do. Like the books at the bookstore. We should have one since we're real authors, too, right?"

Suddenly, a sea of faces looked back at me. I had no choice. They were real authors. Real authors had hard covers, shiny pages, and little letters and numbers in the front. They were right. And I simply had to find a way to ensure that their *Pre-K East Life Book* would be "a really real book."

2. Because the pre-K children had identified the binding as one of the key aspects of a "real book" as they inquired and investigated different books, and because Dana did not know much about binding and how books were bound, she arranged a class visit to a bookbinder. During this visit, the children learned about the bookbinding process, participated in forms of bookbinding, and got to ask questions of a bookbinder. We do not fully discuss this here, but it was an important part of the project.

Figure 8.4. A Book of Memories

This is a book of memories.

A memory is something that you know about from a long time ago. You might forget, but you remember.

Memory is like when you remember something.

A memory is like where if you did something awesome and you always remember it.

It means you remember what you did a long, long time ago.

It's just when you remember something.

The idea of "a really real book" was central to the children's identification of their writing as "official" (Dyson, 1994b) or real. Demonstrating their knowledge of real books in stores and libraries and offering key concepts about print (Clay, 2000), the children asserted their expertise, using it to support their accompanying conclusions. In order to be real authors, their book needed a particular shape, smell, and texture. It had to have a copyright date and place. Dana acknowledged the truth in what they said and set about finding a way to make it possible within the limited budget that had been allocated to her classroom for supplies.

After researching many different online possibilities, Lucinda discovered the website Blurb (www.blurb.com), which published photo books and allowed her to upload the many images and words of the children into a small book. The teachers' commitment to communicating with the children meant that they were engaging the children in the economics of publishing. The teachers explained that although their book would look like a real book, it would likely be much smaller than the books displayed on the classroom shelves because of cost. Unless they wanted to have one bigger book for the entire class, individual books would require a smaller size. The children understood the relationship between cost and size as well as the relationship between total cost and the classroom budget. They were then okay with smaller books.

The books arrived a few weeks before the end of school. They came in a big brown box, which the teachers placed in the center of the carpet. Together, the children looked at the address for the sender, and talked about where the box came from. Then they unwrapped the box, finding the books inside. "Real books!" Simon exclaimed.

Nestled inside the books were 20 copies of *The Pre-K East Life Book*—shiny, with stiff covers, small writing, "and that book smell" we all love. The official shape of *The Pre-K East Life Book* was important, not only to the children, but to the larger world. Of all the books created that semester, this is the only one that still sits on the coffee table in the school office. It is a beautiful, "official" representation of the children's work . . . even 3 years later.

It was important to honor the vision that the children had, not only for their integrity, but also because of the integrity of the work—because they were right. "Really real books" are different from homemade books; they greet the world with a different voice and put a different face on our work and lives.

A Motley Collection

As the memories for *The Pre-K East Life Book* were compiled, the teachers were faced with a conundrum. They recognized that, as teachers, they are perhaps prone to prioritize organization and abide by particular constructs of equality. If one child makes a picture, shouldn't every child? If one tells a story, certainly all should tell stories. If a photo memory of one child is included, surely every child should have a photo memory. These were the queries that emerged as Dana and Lucinda worked with the children on this book. Yet this quest for sameness often obscures the importance of equity: an equality of possible outcomes (Souto-Manning, 2013). In the case of *The Pre-K East Life Book*, equity meant inclusion of important stories.

As a result, Dana and Lucinda soon realized that the structure and organization of a typical class book simply was not there. It couldn't be. This was not a class book; it was a "really real book." It was comprised of the children's memories, and they simply could not be corralled into any sense of sameness or standardization. After all, they were not the same; although the children were members of the Pre-K East community, they were also individuals with unique experiences and memories. As such, their voices, perspectives, and points of view needed to be honored. There were stories of monkey bar challenges, of the building of booby traps, of meeting one another for the first time, and of the birth of friendships. These were the threads that fashioned a community committed to fairness and democratic processes.

As a result, the book contained stories about the stories that were told. There were also pictures of the classroom community at play and drawings of children's ideas and accomplishments. There was layer upon layer of whom they were as a community and how that community had been established, cultivated, and evolved over the course of the pre-K year. There were memories told by one author, but then enriched as another voice that joined in on the memory. The structure of a traditional class book or any sense of equality simply would not hold.

As the teachers tried to make sense of this new book, they finally realized that this difference was exactly what made the book *The Pre-K East Life Book*. Just as children's lives and memories were not the same and did not follow an exact format, nor should this book. What emerged was a varied collection of voices, stories, memories, drawings, and images of the children and the many ways they remembered themselves both individually and as a collective. It truly was a *Life Book*.

As this book you are reading goes to print to become a "real" book, these same children are on their way to 5th grade. And as Dana rereads *The Pre-K East Life Book*, she can still remember them, hear their daily dramas and quirks in her ears. Their book brings them back to Dana again and again; Simon was right. As she leafs through the pages, she can never forget their "do you remember" stuff, as she reminisces about the history of this classroom community.

CONCLUSION OF THIS CHAPTER AND OF PART II

In this chapter, we unveiled the intricate relationship of social studies learning and The Book Project within the context of the Pre-K East classroom. Centering the voices of pre-K children and the processes undertaken by them, we unveiled how family history was invited into the curriculum as every family shared stories from "when-I-was-little," later authored by the pre-K children in their *A Book of Family Shares*. We also explained how *The Pre-K East Life Book* emerged from an enthusiastic culture circle in which children reflected their need to share memories of the past year with the rest of the world and to document their history as a community, "so other kids can know how to be in our class like we are." As we did so, we offered concrete examples of how social studies can come to life meaningfully within the context of a child-centered pre-K classroom.

Through reading this and the other chapters that comprise Part II of this book, we hope that you can recognize how The Book Project was a site where children's interests were honored, their questions were centered, and the curriculum was authentically integrated, bringing multiple disciplines or content areas together. Each of the books we shared in Part II (as well as the others produced in the context of this study but not shared here) reflected both individuals and the community identity as a whole, questions the children had about the world, and ways of situating themselves in that world. Through authoring a variety of books, the pre-K children engaged in reading, authoring, and storytelling as the creation of an "official" space for the self within their classroom (Dyson, 1994a). They also engaged in learning about the arts (visual and verbal), mathematics and science, and social studies in meaningful and authentic ways — in ways that honored young children as capable learners and positioned them as curriculum coconstructors.

Part III

Reflecting on The Book Project in the Larger Context of Teaching and Learning

In Part III, we take a step back from The Book Project to look at the perspectives, impacts, and implications of this kind of work. Although this book gives an intimate telling of one classroom story, we want to make visible how this small story can be about all of us. While this curriculum and these precise experiences are not presented so they can be replicated, the intentions and perspectives behind the work are available to all of us as practitioners, teachers of teachers, and administrators. As such, we hope that this work sheds light onto and inspires transformations in the shape of the literacy curriculum in early childhood classrooms across time and space.

We take a step back to explore the broader perspective of what has been represented in this one classroom project. We address the realities of the teacher and the skills and conceptual understandings that emerge and are deepened when children are immersed in this kind of work, as well as the social implications of this kind of work on a classroom community. Thus, the two chapters in Part III address the "so what?" of this work for teaching and learning with young children during a time in which early childhood education has experienced increased investments leading to the push down of academics and heightened scrutiny. Showcasing different voices and experiences, we step back and offer reflections.

In Chapter 9 we look at several different elements (the teacher, the child, the community), hoping to unveil the "so-what-ness" of this work. In doing so, we consider how one small story can become a valuable tool for *all* teachers . . . and for you, who are reading this book. We hope that by naming the world of the Pre-K East class and its intricacies, as seen by children and adults, we are able to inspire you—and to remind ourselves—to transform our own worlds. In Chapter 10, we have the opportunity to look back with the children of The Book Project several years later. We look at memory, wondering about what has been learned and what the children carry with them as they move forward through their schooling experience. Through conversations with teachers and current pre-K students, the older alumni from The Book Project offer their insightful perspectives and important memories.

CHAPTER 9

Perspectives and Insights on Authorship in an Emergent, Child-Centered Classroom

Teacher Nightmares and Having Faith

It is late August, and I am setting up my classroom, racing off to faculty meetings, laminating name cards, trying to find the other half of the Magna-Tile collection, which has somehow gone missing, and wondering about the origins of the mysterious smell that seems to be coming from the back of the supply closet. Several email addresses on my class list seem to be incorrect, and my parent emails keep bouncing back. I need to make new schedule cards, and I am a whirling dervish of stress. It's that time of year when I keep starting a job, then another, then another, ultimately realizing that I am simultaneously working on six half-finished projects and completing none of them. You would think, after 17 years, that I would have a better system. I do not.

And the underlying fear, beneath all this laminating, labeling, and organizing, is: What if it doesn't work this time? What if there isn't a common interest? What if a project doesn't emerge? What if I don't help them get the skills and develop the concepts that they need? And with that fear is the almost overwhelming desire to make a plan—to simply fix this.

It would be so easy to just make a binder, to get out a planner, to organize the curriculum, and to know, to be sure, of where it is going. In just a few days, young children will walk through my classroom door, waiting for me to teach them, to tell them, to make them safe. Their parents are likely to be asking the same questions. They have the same uncertainty: "Where are you going, and what are you doing?" they ask with their eyes, their hand on their child's shoulder, a complete juxtaposition of parent certitude and total insecurity as they worry for their child. I could allay all these fears. If I only would make a binder filled with lesson and unit plans spanning the entire year. . . . But then I would compromise my faith in young children and my knowledge that the curriculum needs to be coconstructed with them, not by me for them. After all, teaching is not the transmission of knowledge, but the development of humanity.

We opened this section with this story because we think it is important that you know that this work can be scary. We know that we are making assumptions about teachers, about who you are as a teacher, but we are going to assume that many of you are like Dana. You are organizers. You are planners. You are the people who make everything all right. When there is a crisis, you are the ones in charge, directing people, grabbing first-aid kits, calling parents, and never letting on how worried or frightened you might be. This is what you do as an early childhood teacher. Your job is to make everything all right.

We shared this brief story above because we want you to know that this work is not easy for Dana either. She has to wrestle with these demons, year after year, to test her faith in the children and their ability to lead her toward something better than any predetermined curriculum. We want you to know that if you are anything like her, the fear does not go away. The impulse to organize and fix does not dissipate. The shift—from wanting to be in control to sharing the power with young children—only starts to happen when you focus on the power and possibility of the work, reflecting on and relearning from the experiences you have *with* the children.

Over the years, as you try and try again, you will collect a host of experiences, of rich work born of coconstructing curriculum with the children. These memories and the traces they leave behind must become your metaphorical binders. It is in these experiences that you can find calm and solace when the urge to control comes over you, because these stories will tell you again and again that this is possible. They offer evidence of the power and possibility of a critical emergent curriculum cogenerated by young children. It will happen. Your job is not to make the curriculum, but to set up the environment, the structures and frameworks, in which that curriculum might happen. And that is where your energies should go, in those early days of newness and insecurity.

When you make the choice to allow the curriculum to grow out of the children, to learn to see who they are and where that might take you, this choice challenges you to let go of some control. In fact, teachers sometimes have to let things go "all wrong" before they finally emerge as all right (remember the sand-clogged sink?). You really have to get comfortable with being uncomfortable. It is in this discomfort that you can begin to create the space where authentic ideas can be born. When you allow the trouble to happen, when you rely on the children to come up with the answers, you start building the space in which the real work can begin. But you cannot do the work until you create that space, and the space is made of stepping back and supporting the children in becoming leaders, questioners, and problem-solvers. Dana loves to solve problems. We imagine that you do, too. But it is so much more satisfying to be the person who teaches the children to solve problems themselves.

The culture circle framework we explained and presented in Chapter 1 fosters such a development. Within the culture circle framework (Freire, 1970; Souto-Manning, 2010), children are socialized into reading their worlds ethnographically, identifying pressing and oppressing issues (generative themes), troubling the roots of such issues (problematization), engaging in a process whereby they dialogue and learn from and with one another. This is the process that leads to problem solving and to action. As a teacher, Dana carefully documents students' process through project work (also explained in Chapter 1), amassing evidence of their learning and coming to better support them.

In a book about pre-K stories, have we strayed from a focus on literacy? The truth is, the thinking, the process, the stories, the selves, are the center of the work you do as a literacy teacher, supporting young children's development as authors who are knowledgeable about literacy across content areas. But how do children arrive at the work? How are they positioned as literate? Do they enter this work empty, looking to the teacher to lead and fill them? Or are they challenged to think differently, to lead where they might have followed, to see themselves as rich resources rather than empty vessels? Often, literacy work—its traditional practices, rituals, and routines—seems so distant from who young children really are. But it shouldn't be. As the International Literacy Association (2018) recently defined: "Literacy is the ability to identify, understand, interpret, create, compute, and communicate using visual, audible, and digital materials across disciplines and in any context." Literacy thus "connects people to one another and empowers them to achieve things they never thought possible." From this definition, the work of this book is literacy.

When you understand what literacy is from this broad and expansive perspective and when you make the body of the classroom, the habits you form, the questions you ask, the messages you write, and the curricula you pursue, when you make all of that *about* the children, when you make the classroom *with* them, you reshape their paths into literacies. You invite their individual values, their stories, their questions, and their very selves to be the center of the curriculum and the content of their literacies. You position them as capable authors.

We want to take a moment to talk about and rethink what counts as teaching, facilitating, and leadership in the early childhood classroom, because all too often, this kind of work gets dismissed as unstructured, without goals, or disorganized in some way. We would like to be clear and say that this kind of work with children requires a much higher level of organization, facilitation, and leadership than we ever before had to exercise when we were doing more traditional, teacher-directed work. You are not at liberty to sit back and simply allow the work to unfold. You are the facilitator of the unfolding. It is up to you as the teacher to listen closely to every comment, to knit them together in a way that makes sense, to tell the story back to the children so that they can see the curriculum becoming, and to move forward in constructing cohesive goals, which allow them to meet (and often surpass) expectations set forth for their learning. It is also your responsibility to hear the voices that are not being heard, to find ways to integrate all voices into the curriculum, and to ensure that all areas of the curriculum are meaningfully brought together.

As you do this work, you will find that you are always planning, webbing possibilities, thinking of how the coconstructed curriculum might evolve, and then rerouting when the children take a detour (some of these result in big shifts in learning journeys, as seen in Part II of this book). In the midst of this vortex of planning and scaffolding, you are also responsible for the development of skills and concepts that children need to learn—those that populate the pages of binders, often handed to you by the administration. With them in mind, but centering children's priorities, questions, and experiences, you should think carefully about what the children need to know, finding the spaces where that can enter the work, making room so that the children will be prepared for the next step . . . all while honoring who they are, their questions, and their interests.

In doing this work, you will identify the threads that comprise the fabric of the classroom community, weave the classroom community, and then guide the unfolding of learning. You will lead from the sidelines, stepping back when the children take the reins and sailing back in when support is needed. You will embrace what Vygotsky (1978) long ago called scaffolding, and foster—with the children—zones of proximal development, where children can develop beyond their level of independent work, with assistance from a more knowledgeable other—an adult or another child. This is complex work. It entails social mediation. It is also the most exhilarating and satisfying work we have ever done. It is, from our perspective, theory-generating practice, coconstructed *with* young children. It reclaims the early childhood education classroom as a site where knowledge is produced, where theories are generated, as Dana reflects below.

Teacher Nightmares and Having Faith (Continued)

It has now been a few years since The Book Project unfolded in my pre-K classroom, and I still look at the collection of works with awe. I wondered, when we started writing this book, if I would remember, if I had enough documentation to write authentically about this class and its work. I shouldn't have worried. This set of works and the documentation of The Book Project is just teeming with the voices of the children.

As I reread my notes and engage in the process of writing, I can hear them shouting out the trajectory of their airplanes, calling for the exact color of pink for Barbie's car, and whispering a quiet family apple-picking story. They correct me as I write, insisting that I tell their real story, in all its messiness.

And as I look back at this work and its richness, I have faith again—faith that this work can happen, will happen, over and over again in different ways, if we just allow it to happen just as it has over the past few years . . . in unique and child-centered ways, in ways that honor young children's questions, experiences, interests, expertise, and priorities.

The voices of young children and the images of their experiences once again provide me with the necessary assurance. And now, even in my beginning-of-the-year panic, the power, possibility, and purpose of this work become once again so much clearer.

EXPLORING CHILDREN'S DEVELOPMENT OF TRADITIONAL LITERACY SKILLS

In this section, we reflect on the ways that child-centered literacy work changes children's perspectives on language arts, writing, publishing, and expression. Through an intimate view of the classroom, we examine the ways that young children can be motivated and electrified by work that is so deeply, authentically theirs. In doing so, we reflect on the affordances of problem-posing literacy education (Freire, 1970)—education whereby teachers pose problems as opposed to rushing to solve them—for children's learning and development, particularly as it relates to children's spelling of words.

"How Do You Know How to Write Words?"

When the connection between play and storytelling took hold, I became a very busy scribe. There was something so miraculous about a wonderful animal game or a particularly dramatic shark attack in the unit block area being set down on paper, appearing as words to be kept for all time. The children swarmed around Lucinda and me, begging us, "Write down my story!"

Soon, lines formed and frustration built. I took to writing stories out on my computer because I can type faster than I can write.

Then came the clamoring for trips to the printer so that the children could actually hold the written stories in their hands. It was a self-created problem, I will admit, and a good problem to have. It's just that Lucinda and I weren't getting much done beyond story writing.

We also knew that we wanted the children to have other options, to know that adults were not the only keepers of the written word. Thus, we presented the problem at morning meeting. Our message said:

Good morning, Pre-K East!

We are noticing that many people want to write stories. Sometimes, the teachers write the stories down on paper, but there aren't enough teachers to do all the writing. We have big lines, and sometimes kids' stories don't get written down. We have some questions for you:

- *What can we do?*
- *How do you know how to write words?*

Love,
Dana and Lucinda

The meeting was filled with immediate responses to the problem. We had many "experts" on the writing of letters, as well as many children with theories about how this might be possible. Some jumped in immediately, sharing information they had used in their past writing, while other children took a moment, thinking of the different ways to navigate the journey from the sound of a word to its representation in letters. Their hands raised, some quickly, and others with thoughtful deliberation. The children offered their ideas:

- You just listen to the word and then you can hear the letters.
- Sometimes that is tricky but you say the words really slow. Stretch them. Then you can hear the letters. Like this: "sssssss-lllll-ooooo-wwwww." Then you can hear them all.
- You can ask me and I can help you!
- Yeah, the teachers, but also some of the kids can help spell things.
- Sometimes it doesn't really matter if you spelled it with the right letters as long as the letters make the right sounds. Like, *C* and *S* can make the same sound.

This conversation opened up so many possibilities in our work. From the children, we heard about how one can find and identify the letters in the word. We identified some "experts," who were happy to help their classmates with this work. We also made an important discovery about spelling: It doesn't matter if it's "right." It just matters if "the letters make the right sounds." This theory, offered by a child, pushed back against so many of those "real school" worries about "doing it right" that can often make the kids give up before they have even begun.

Following this conversation, new writing erupted in the classroom, and questions about the sounds in words became as frequent as requests for "Will you write down my story?"

Our authoring had texture. It was scribed. It was comprised of invented spelling. It encompassed stories told through illustrations. It included spoken stories woven into block structures. Our classroom was alive with story, and the children could see their own textured authorship coming to life in a wide gamut of literacies.

We share the above story because it demonstrates a natural way in which work pertaining to traditional literacy skills can become essential and alive in the life of young children when it is authentic and serves a purpose (Lindfors, 2008). The children in the Pre-K East class were not questioning the "whys" of listening for letter sounds. Dana did not sit them down and insist that they go through a mini-lesson on this work, proceeding from demonstration to shared practice, guided practice, and independent practice, according to what has been labeled the "optimal learning model," characterized by the gradual handover of responsibilities from teacher to student (Routman, 2003).

The need for the development of traditional literacy skills presented itself within the curriculum, and the children knew why. They were not questioning, for example, why they were learning to identify chunks in words or why they should care about the difference between a question mark and an exclamation point. They knew that chunks in known words could help them spell new words in their stories. They knew that from the word *bite*, they could write *kite* or *site*, engaging with *onsets* (the beginning sound before the vowel) and *rimes* (the letters that follow) to help children write new words[1] (Souto-Manning & Martell, 2016). They also knew that in their stories, it mattered whether their characters were asking a question or declaring something.

The children's learning of traditional literacy skills was informed and guided by their sense of urgency—by their purpose to communicate meaning, to author stories. It was because they were authors, because they had stories to tell, because the teachers could not do all of the writing themselves. The teachers needed help solving a problem in the classroom—the problem of writing down stories as fast as they were being authored.

There is power in telling the truth, in making problems visible to young children and allowing them to solve them. This is called problem-posing education. It is a powerful, critical approach to teaching and learning that positions children agentively (Freire, 1970). One of the most powerful elements of this practice is the way in which children offer solutions for addressing identified problems. And in doing so, they are committed to being part of the action, of the solution to the problem posed.

The problem Dana and Lucinda had posed empowered the pre-K children to realize the need for more traditional literacy skills. They themselves

---

1. For example, for the word *sun*, *s* would be the onset and *un* would be the rime. Knowledge of onset and rimes can be important for writing because approximately "500 words can be derived from 37 rimes" (Souto-Manning & Martell, 2016, p. 89).

had identified the need to develop their fine motor skills, the need to independently hear the sounds in words, the need to order their writing so that the story would be told correctly. They were not doing the work "because my teacher told me to." They were doing the work—developing fine motor skills, graphophonic knowledge (letter–sound or symbol–sound correspondence), and knowledge of punctuation—because they were writing stories they had authored. Some were developing orthographic knowledge as they experimented with writing, attending to "the configuration of letters, directionality, punctuation (including segmentation)" (Owocki & Goodman, 2002, p. 81). Others were attending "to the way print looked," writing with curves and lines to make symbols intended to carry meaning (p. 81). The children in Pre-K East were engaging their full linguistic repertoires to make meaning.

As Freppon and Dahl (1991) documented decades ago, children develop knowledge of phonics—and of other traditional literacy skills—in the context of authentic language experiences, including reading and writing. And teachers can support such development, which involves identifying, leveraging, cultivating, and expanding the skills children bring with them to the classroom. This is best done when teachers recognize that the best way to learn about what young children know and can do is to observe and document their engagement in a variety of meaningful experiences and processes, including play (Owocki & Goodman, 2002).

Yet the acquisition and development of these skills do not happen in a void. Teachers must be part of the process, supporting young children in developing and discovering these abilities and skills in themselves. Dana does this work through the physical and interactional design of her pre-K classroom (frequently exemplified earlier in this book):

- Ensuring the meaningful inclusion of written language throughout the classroom (labeling cubbies with pictures and symbols, having a displayed schedule that children can decode, using morning messages to communicate something meaningful, having books and other printed materials available throughout the classroom)
- Asking meaningful and authentic questions about words, letters, and sounds in the flow of the day (for example, when writing an unfamiliar word or proper name, inquiring out loud where that information may be found and then demonstrating how books, labels, and other printed materials can serve as resources for writing)
- Coauthoring letters to be sent to families with children, communicating that writing serves a communicative purpose (for example, refer to the letter inviting families to share stories, Figure 8.1)
- Transcribing children's stories, authored in and through play

- Interactively writing with children (sharing the pen or the marker)
- Noticing and noting features of texts in read-alouds
- Engaging in think-alouds (making connections between words, noting onsets and rimes)
- Using child-made labels with a variety of symbols (pictures, symbols, words in languages spoken by the children) throughout the classroom
- Inviting children to develop a system to classify and label their work

All of these small actions help reveal to the children how language works in general—and how written language works in particular. Although not prescriptive or all-encompassing, these are some of the ways in which teachers can seek to foster a language- and literacy-rich pre-K classroom. When Dana integrates these experiences into the everydayness of her pre-K class, the children develop knowledge that reveals itself when they take these first independent steps as writers. They find that the knowledge is there, lurking beneath the surface, ready to be picked up and tested through a number of hypotheses.

Dana and Lucinda are also strategic in the questions they ask (many of them visible in the morning messages and stories shared in this book) and in the way these questions guide the work of the project. They know that they want the children to develop these literacy skills at their own pace. Honoring their individual timelines means that teachers listen closely, document carefully, and ask questions that help bring out children's thoughts and theories about how language in general and written language in particular work. These discussions, conducted within culture circles and pertaining to topics and questions that matter to the children, ignite their interest in writing. It is within this context that the children lay claim to traditional literacy skills, and the need for them, within their work in the classroom. This happens year after year.

Although these skills are vital to the children, they are not just "skills." They are tools for making meaning in the social world. They allow for communicating particular ways of being and become essential for who children are becoming as authors, allowing them to develop ownership and express themselves in more nuanced ways in the world. The amazing thing about this perspective on the acquisition and development of traditional literacy skills by young children, typically taught through direct instruction, is that teachers are reminded of the power of a child-centered, emergent, critical curriculum. There is no resistance, no feeling of inadequacy, no pressure. The children fully embrace and own the development of these skills, at times testing a never-ending number of hypotheses.

In the Pre-K East class, children develop their writing of letters, of letter-like symbols, and of pictorial representations side by side. They learn to make meaning on paper with a multitude of symbolic representations. Their symbols are valued and their confidence grows. At their own pace, they progress toward the acquisition and development of writing—letters, words, sentences, and stories—through traditional spelling and approximations. As teachers set up classrooms that support children as authors, as meaning-makers, and eventually as writers, we get to be a part of that. We witness the miracle of being part of the children's becoming—developing their humanity.

Through the many questions and discussions that permeated Pre-K East, it became clear to Dana that the children saw an overwhelming purpose to their authorship. And they regarded spelling, writing words, as an essential pathway to authoring written stories. "It's so that people can see what we can do!" one of them explained. This manifested itself in a wide range of "seeings." Collectively, the pre-K learning community went from documenting memories, to sharing family stories, to making sure that others could learn the deft skills of making a paper airplane. Now, the children were engaging in making meaning and making sense with growing independence. They were communicating their experiences, sharing their expertise, and writing themselves in the world without fully depending on their teachers.

All of this work was ultimately about seeing and being seen, about making visible the people that they became and the abilities that they developed. This is a serious goal, a profound goal, and one that embeds the act of authorship with powerful meaning. This goal, this need to know and be known, to see and be seen, was the fuel behind each carefully spelled word, each laborious new letter, and each detailed illustration. Their skills and challenges were a part of their *selves*, and the need to make those selves visible to the world, as explained by Marcus (below).

Igniting Invented Spelling

"What are you working on?" I asked Marcus, who was bent over his paper, pencil in hand, whispering to himself. Marcus is an independent worker and likes to conduct his wrestlings with letters in his own space. Yes, I was being annoying.

"I'm just working," he said gruffly, not looking up.

"But what's it about?" I asked, undeterred. Marcus and I have a longstanding relationship. I've known him since he was 2. He knows he's not escaping this one.

With a big sigh, he turned to me. "It's about when we were in New Hampshire. And we were on the four-wheeler. Out on the ice. Okay?" he asked, hope blooming in his eyes. Maybe I would go away and leave him to his work.

"But it seems like you're doing something with the words," I continued. "How are you making them?"

"Just sounding them out," he said, looking peeved. He knew that I knew exactly what he was doing. What was the point of this conversation?

"But why do you want to write them?" I gave one last try.

"Because then people can know about what we did!" he exclaimed. "And none of them were there. And then I can write it all by myself, and the class and other kids can know my story. Can I write now, please?" he asked, and I stepped away. Often, writing is much more important than talking to teachers.

UNDERSTANDING THE DEVELOPMENT OF A LEARNING COMMUNITY

The work of The Book Project is deeply connected to the idea of community. This particular community on which The Book Project was predicated was comprised of young children who together developed the skills to collaborate, question, support, and create as learners. Community is never a given, but something coconstructed, nurtured, and cultivated across time. And so it was in the Pre-K East class. From its very beginnings, when the kitchen sink was clogged by sand to the time when the children decided to write a book to capture its history, community was always at work, at the center of the pre-K class. The members of the community fostered in the Pre-K East classroom recognized that there was more expertise distributed than in any one member (Ladson-Billings, 2012)—and so did Dana and Lucinda as teachers. The children knew that they were stronger and better together.

In this section, we reflect on the communities created through this work and the communities that allow this kind of work to develop. As we connect the intimacy of classroom stories to broader concepts important to early childhood classroom communities, we hope to offer insights that inform the development of learning communities in your own setting.

"It's Better If We Put Our Stories Together"

"Mmmmm," Simon said, frowning, looking this way and that at his paper. He was clearly dissatisfied, and I was bemused. His story, "Ninjas," was dramatic and well written, complete with shark biting, screaming, and the requisite drama of 5-year-old writing. The illustration contained a shark with teeth, as well as screaming ninjas, with word bubbles calling "AAAAAAH!" It was excellent work in my opinion, and I told him so.

Simon is not one to be persuaded by the mere opinion of his teacher. He has bigger things on his mind than pleasing me, and he faintly responded to my praise, clearly deep in thought. "It's just too little," he said. "It's like, only one page. And it's only about one thing."

"Yeah," added Margo, who was working on her own creation, "Animals Make Friends," at the table as well. "Some people in our class play ninjas. But not everybody. Some people don't like that game."

"And," added Simon, gaining momentum, "books are supposed to have lots of pages! We're reading that real chapter book, *Mr. Popper's Penguins*, and it has lots of pages and chapters!"

"Well," I chimed in, "what do you want to do?"

Margo and Simon looked at each other again, but did not speak. Sometimes there is this silent talk, these looks that speak to each other, as these two did. And without words, they arrived at an agreement. I watch those communications, quietly amazed. Sometimes they communicate more in their silence. After a few moments, I could see that the exchange had been completed and they were ready to let me in on the decision.

"It's better if we put the stories together," declared Margo, with authority.

"Yes," added Simon, "then it can be for the whole pre-K and it will have lots of pages and chapters. We can talk about it at meeting."

"Yeah, so everyone can know about it and make their own story," added Margo.

"Then we can put us all together and it can be the whole book," Simon concluded seriously, looking to make sure that I had the right level of solemnity.

"Okay," I agreed, "that sounds like a plan," thinking we were done.

"Um, Dana?" asked Margo, with a tiny, underlying hint of attitude in her voice. "Can you write that on the board? Like, in the schedule? Because you know, you forget things sometimes."

"Good point," I said, sighing. "The dry-erase markers are over there on the shelf. Why don't you guys go write it into the schedule?"

They marched off, filled with purpose. "You can spell it and I can write it!" declared Margo, the two making sure that our "whole" book would not be forgotten. This simple, intimate conversation between two children was a foundation for the collaborative work we would do as a class. Their intense communication, followed by "making it official" on our classroom schedule, provided a space in which collective work would emerge. Through the children's making sense of books and how they are constructed, we wound our way toward the first book in The Book Project.

In the Pre-K East classroom, writing and authorship have always been characterized by this sense of "wholeness." There is this sense of taking pieces of ourselves and putting them together to make something more, something that more wholly represents the community. This was Dana's favorite part of this project—the idea that through writing, they were becoming a community, becoming more fully a "we." Anne Haas Dyson and Celia Genishi (1994), who gave us the words and the compass that guide this discussion, explained: "Within and through stories, we fashion our relationships with others, joining with them, separating from them, expressing in ways subtle and not so subtle our feelings about the people around us" (p. 3). They go on to explain storytelling and making as the creators of new "wes" and cultures in the classroom. This captures the establishment and development of community in the Pre-K East class.

Through stories, the Pre-K East class was putting itself together, making itself as a community, and then making that community visible. The children were (re)making themselves from a collection of individuals into a "we"—a "we" with stories, with adventures, with questions, and with responsibilities. They were making a "we" with collective goals, which required the participation of everyone in order to make it whole. Most important, the children were authoring themselves into a "we," into a safe space to take risks and grow, an interconnected system, unique and completely whole.

As you consider and reflect on The Book Project and the many works created in this process, we ask you to take a step away from the skills it fostered and the literacy goals it achieved. For a moment, we ask you to think about the relationships that were cultivated and developed. Take a moment to consider the "wes" that were created and how these relationships and varied communities served the children. There was the "we" of the class, the "we" of the Pre-K East community, which was the most essential goal in this work. There were also the smaller "wes" created through small-group work, from coauthoring stories, to the collaborative storytelling of dramatic play, to the experimentation and documentation of small-group work in *The Book of Paper Airplane Experts*. There was the "we" of families as the children invited their home lives and memories into the classroom through *A Book of Family Shares*. There were the "wes" of children outside the Pre-K East classroom; through their writing, they taught others and shared knowledge.

It is through the lenses of "we" that teachers can come to understand young "children as individuals who bring with them stories meant to be lived out with others" (Souto-Manning & Yoon, 2018, p. 23). To do so, it becomes necessary to understand literacy relationally. Relational literacies "imply the labor of making meaning, of shared knowledges, or of producing and developing new knowledges together" (Licona & Chávez, 2015, p. 96). Relational literacies "are never produced singularly or in isolation but rather depend on interaction" (p. 96). They are produced within the context of "wes" of the present and of the future as the children remembered their stories, conceptualizing themselves as a community, purposefully leaving a trace of the "we" they created, knowing that change would soon come.

When children develop relational literacies, when they learn to honor their relationships, when they practice "wholeness," when they say, "It's better if we put our stories together," they are developing the skills to create something better than what we have now in the world. In such communities, children develop new kinds of understanding, of interacting, of learning, and of growing. They engage with "the desire and possibility for shared action" (Licona & Chávez, 2015, p. 96) and for coconstructed meaning-making.

In and through authoring communities, the young children in the Pre-K East class positioned "community histories as meaningful" (Licona & Russell, 2013, p. 2) in their *Pre-K East Life Book*. Through the sharing of individual stories in books such as *The Whole Pre-K East Book*, they wrote as a community in ways that made "people and places knowable and understandable" (Licona & Russell, 2013, p. 2). Through the writing of "wes," they fostered the development of a powerful community—a diverse and ever-changing community.

Even before moving on to kindergarten, the children in Dana's class realized that their community was always being authored and reauthored, written and rewritten. Together, they realized new "wes" as they learned, grew, and developed together . . . within and beyond the boundaries of the Pre-K East classroom.

Authorship and the Making of Us

It's almost 2 years after The Book Project, and my Pre-K East classroom is full of a motley crew of different ages. We are doing our winter "mix-up" time, when a mix of pre-K, kindergarten, and 1st-graders are all mixed and visit different classrooms for playtime. It's a special time for me as my "big kids" come back home to their old classroom and multiple ages come together for play. It's amazing to me how they quickly gather on the purple carpet again, remembering the details of their old stories, sharing this kind of communion of young and "old" (read: ages 6 and 7) through their layered histories in this room.

On this day, Peter and Clay headed over to the Cozy Corner with a clear sense of trouble bubbling from their bodies. It was freezing and snowy outside, they hadn't been able to go out for outdoor play, and they were ready to do some body tumbling in a space that no longer fit their bodies. I stood just close enough to the space to intercede if there was tumbling furniture, but far enough away for them to proceed with their pillow-throwing, rough-and-tumble mischief. A small pillow flew through the air and knocked the books off of the shelf. On top of the tumbled pile was a laminated copy of *The Book of Paper Airplane Experts*.

"Hey!" cried Clay, plopping down on the floor. "Remember this?"

Peter immediately joined him, and they thumbed through the pages, looking at their writing and their pictures and remembering their stories. They were soon joined by other children in the classroom, all interested in this book about "the big boys."

"Can you teach us to make these?" asked Harry, tentative but infatuated by these big guys and their work.

"Sure! Let's get the paper out," shouted Clay, grabbing the book and leading the group to the back of the room. Soon they were spread out across the art table, looking closely at the book, folding paper, teaching, and remembering. I could see them in my mind's eye, years ago, in the exact same positions, using their book to teach children from the other class.

And here we were, years later, their book still in hand, authoring a new "we" as they took their old work and used it to teach the 1st-graders, kindergartners, and pre-K kids in my classroom that day.

Layers of stories all came to life as they worked, planes once again racing overhead and disturbing the room. And as they headed out to the hallway by the cubbies, "because that's the best place for a runway!" I knew that their stories and the communities they had made were alive and well, disrupting my peaceful classroom once more.

And fashioning yet another "we," they inspired this new pre-K class to write "how-to" books, just like the one they had authored years earlier, when they themselves were in pre-K.

CHAPTER 10

"Look at Us! We're All So Different!"

Remembering and Reflecting 3 Years Later

As we conclude this book about The Book Project and its potential for integrating curriculum in ways that are critical and child-centered, we decided that it was important to ask the children who had been members of Pre-K East years earlier to revisit the books they had authored. In this chapter, Dana speaks about how two of her former students (who were concluding 2nd grade and about to go to 3rd grade at the time they were interviewed) made sense of their experiences (then and now) and of The Book Project.

It is always an intimidating thing to reflect back with students many years later. As teachers, we imagine the impact we may have had. We dream of the futures that the children we taught will find. We hope that we have given them something, offered something eternal, even as sharp memories fade. We accept our transience in children's lives, but hope that we have given them something to carry with them, something they will hold and wield into their futures.

This is why Dana waited so long to conduct these interviews. She reflected:

> I wish I could say that I wanted to give it time, wanted to see what was sustained over many years, but the reality is that I was afraid. I was afraid of being forgotten. I was afraid that our work together, so profound to me, was like water that had slipped away in the fast-flowing river of the children's experience.
>
> This Book Project interview, conducted at the end of the children's 2nd-grade year, is both everything and nothing that I expected it to be. It is, like the children, so deeply them, expected and unexpected, deeply pragmatic and with flashes of poignancy. It is through these moments, these intimidating reckonings of our "impacts," that we see the traces of our teaching, of our project work, emerge, unique, unexpected, and yet entirely present and thriving in the children's lives.

"Don't Step on Anything! 'Cause It Will Break. It's *Really* Old!"

My well-planned interview about The Book Project unfolded in just about the same way that all things do in the life of a pre-K teacher: chaotically. My plan (I always have a plan) had been to pick Susan up from her 2nd-grade classroom right after school, and to sit quietly and thoughtfully, just the two of us in the pre-K room so that she had plenty of time and space for her thoughts. In reality, our time was curtailed by a last-minute faculty meeting and the quiet peace of my classroom was thwarted by several children whose families were late for pickup. I'd also forgotten about Susan's younger sister, Bella (a current student of mine), who was also firmly ensconced in my classroom. She was not about to be left out of this discussion; this was her classroom now.

I raced over to Susan's room and gathered her things, needing to rush back to my classroom where another teacher was keeping an eye on my kids. Susan stepped out with an excited but awkward smile. I felt suddenly nervous at the artificial feeling of the "interview," mirroring Susan's awkward expression.

"Good grief," I thought. "How on Earth is this going to play out?" At the last minute, I decided to also gather Trevor from the other 2nd-grade class across the hall. I had planned to interview them individually, but in the moment, it felt right to have them both.

Trevor scampered out with a mischievous grin, giving me a big hug and nearly plowing Susan over as we began walking.

"Hi, Dana! Hi, Susan! Let's go! It's hot outside! We're having a special snack at aftercare. Why are we doing an 'interview'?" he asked, barely stopping for breath. Here was the dispeller of our awkwardness.

"Well, because I want to know what you think," I said. "I'm writing a book, and it's about your Book Project, so I need to know the things you remember."

Trevor nodded his head, satisfied with that answer. It was always wise for adults to take their lead from what children know.

Suddenly, the awkwardness of the earlier moment was quelled as the two children erupted into conversation over the upcoming ice cream social, and the possibilities for ice cream flavors that might be served. I sighed, and my nervousness began to lift.

When we arrived back in the classroom, two children, Bella and Harry, were left from my current pre-K class. Worried about the ways they might impact the discussion, I began to scramble for possibilities of where I could send them when Susan and Trevor again revised my plans. "Come on, guys!" Trevor said. "Stop running around and sit down on the purple carpet."

"Yeah," added Susan, every inch the big sister. "This is our project from when we were in pre-K. We can show you about it."

"But don't step on anything!" called Trevor, dumping the contents of my Book Project folder unceremoniously onto the floor, "'cause it will break. It's *really* old!

Awed by the glow of seniority from the big kids, Bella and Harry sat down obediently. Trevor and Susan looked on them with calm confidence. They were ready to teach.

There is something about the unexpected ways in which the interview unfolded that was essential with regard to how the children engaged in their reflections. Looking back on the day, the first moment of divergence was perhaps the most important. When Susan left her classroom with that awkward smile, I could feel the disingenuousness of the moment. Never had we ever operated in this way while we were in the classroom together. All of our work was conducted as a group; all the books were discussed, negotiated, and emerged from our collective identity. To take those relationships out of the discussion was to lose the center of the project as a whole. The moment we rerouted, collecting Trevor from his classroom, the sense of the work changed, returning back to itself. Perhaps this was not the entire class, but here was someone with whom to remember, someone who shared the stories and the experiences. We needed the dynamic nature of the shared memory.

The presence of the younger children in the classroom was also an unplanned, yet fortuitous circumstance. As seen in the narrative, Susan and Trevor were empowered by the presence of the younger children, instantly transforming into leaders and teachers. They immediately took charge of the space, finding voice through their identity as experienced elders in our school community.

This is not to say that we should always deviate from our plans, just that deviations can sometimes be welcome circumstances. And, as always, it was in these relationships between the children that the deep work emerged. My teacher instinct to organize, to limit the number of children, to limit the mayhem, was inauthentic. It diverged from the typical cacophony from which The Book Project itself emerged. It was only with the return of our usual mayhem that a "real" interview could be found.

Memories of The Book Project

The little group settled down and began paging through the books strewn on the carpet. Based on their very different interests, I had expected that they would gravitate toward different books, but the group traveled together, opening the pages of *A Book of Family Shares.* Trevor and Susan held up the book together, ensconced in their teacher role.

"These are books that we made when we were younger and in pre-K, just like you," Susan began, her voice taking on the sing-songy tone of "playing teacher."

"In this classroom," Trevor added, to avoid confusion. Years may have passed, but this remained "his" classroom. They moved on through the pages, exclaiming over the drawings, their friends, and their memories.

"We're bigger now," began Susan.

"*Much* bigger," clarified Trevor.

"Look at us!" Susan added. "We're all so different!"

"Yeah! You're super big!" Harry affirmed with a worshipful smile.

"I spelled it wrong. We spelled everything wrong!" Trevor said again and again, assuring us all of his current ability to spell it all right.

"Yeah, and look at my hair!" added Susan. When no one noticed anything in particular about her hair, she tried again. "And nothing is spelled right!" she exclaimed, to better response. Soon we came upon Susan's page in the book.

"Look at mine! Ooh—I still do this!" she cried. "I remember that I said that every year in the fall we pick apples at an orchard. Our family is friends with people who own the orchard, and we go there every year, and it's really fun. My favorite part is going on this ride, and it goes through the apple orchard!"

I remember this story, too. Susan taught us all the correct way to twist and pull an apple when picking it. To this day, I think of her every time I pick an apple. As she reflected on this story, her face lit up with the same enthusiasm as when she was 4, sharing with us for the first time. Her world-weary, correct-spelling, 2nd-grader cool fell away, and there was the Susan I knew, bubbling over with the excitement of her annual apple-picking trip.

The Book of Paper Airplane Experts suddenly caught Trevor's eye, and he dropped his side of our *Book of Family Shares*.

"I remember when we did that with the airplanes!" he exclaimed, perusing the pictures. "Look at the Big Blocks room! Look how small it is! Come on! Let's go look."

He jumped up and raced into our Big Blocks play space, followed by both younger children, eager to show off what was now their classroom. Susan stayed seated, a look of reticence on her face. "I'll just stay here with you," she said. "It probably looks different."

Trevor came charging back and flopped onto the purple carpet. "It's so much smaller now!" he announced, followed by the two younger children, awed at anyone who could think that *Big* Blocks was small.

"I remember we were doing airplanes in Big Blocks," Trevor continued. "They didn't know how to make one, so I made one for them, I think."

"Remember?" added Susan. "You showed us the movie of your dad making one on the big screen! That's how we learned how."

"Oh, yeah!" continued Trevor, enthusiastic about being remembered. "You [Dana] said we were allowed to go in there and throw them because,

because—weeelll—we could throw them in Big Blocks, but they would crash. People were walking outside in the hall, and they could step on them. Maybe they didn't understand what we were working on. But you did, so you said we could fly them in the hallway."

I recall this time well, a battle with outside forces over the undesirability of young children flying airplanes in the hallway and my insistence that they needed the space to measure the length of the flight. I feel lucky that this was Trevor's memory of me: someone who allowed, someone who understood.

These reflections illustrate a process of stepping back and remembering ourselves, finding ourselves in the memories of others. The children held themselves at a distance initially, making clear how they had grown. They made careful observations about the growth of their skills, the growth of their bodies, the distance between them now and the children represented in the Pre-K East books. They looked to us, the younger children and me, for our acknowledgment of the distance they had traveled, the growth they had made. Our awareness and respect were reflected back at them. We knew; they had grown up.

There was an essential intersection that occurred between our assurance that we knew Trevor and Susan were "big" and their recognition of themselves and of their stories as they reviewed the books. When they encountered themselves, their experiences, their stories in these books, suddenly the weight of being "big" was shed, and those children who populated my classroom years ago emerged once again. They were exuberant, remembered sharing, bubbling not only with their memories but also with being remembered by others. Trevor lit up at Susan's story about his dad.

I was drawn back to my own memories as Trevor remembered my role in the airplane story. Through this process of knowing and being known, of being seen for who they were now and who they had been in pre-K, and how these parts were intermingled, we came together once again. Trevor and Susan crossed the distance back to me, and we were a class once more, exclaiming over apple-picking techniques and the technicalities of airplane folding.

Futures of The Book Project

Time was running short, and with the required faculty meeting looming in my mind, I pulled out my favorite, *The Pre-K East Life Book*. Susan gently took it from my hand. "It has all the . . ." she stopped, breathing quietly.

"All of the pictures of all of us!" Trevor finished for her, looking at our class portraits, grinning on the back cover. Each child is pictured as he or she was in the first days of pre-K, not the formal "school pictures," but with warm, sweaty faces dappled by the light of the playground.

Susan and Trevor opened the book to the inscription, the children's words about the meaning of memories (refer to Figure 8.4). Susan took one side of the book, Trevor carefully held the other, and without a word they began reading the words to us, taking turns with each description of memory. Their two little heads tucked closely together, and I was still, stunned by the sheer beauty of the moment.

The Pre-K East Life Book seemed to demand a different kind of interaction with the children, and they continued to look through and read the pages in concert with one another, laughing quietly, each holding a side, reading to one another.

"Look, this is a story that Dominique wrote about me," Susan said with a smile. "It's from the beginning of school and we were just getting to know each other."

"Oh! This is that story about the monster in the shed! We all were scared of it and different people wrote a story. We kind of all wrote the story because we were all playing it," added Trevor. "Remember? People kept on throwing sticks in the shed and they were disappearing. They said it was the monster getting the sticks in there."

"I almost thought it was real," Susan added sheepishly.

"Maybe there was just a hole on the other side of the shed," Trevor wondered, still trying to solve our shed-monster mystery.

"This is yours!" Susan exclaimed as she came upon Trevor's memory page. "You read yours! Read it out loud! Then I can read mine!"

They continued through the book, reading snippets, caught in the beauty of those moments and these stories. "I think we probably wrote this because everyone wanted to remember the great stories we had," Susan reflected.

Then, tentatively, Trevor suggested, "Dana, maybe I could bring in my binder thing that has a picture of me now on it and you could show it to people so they know when they read this book. So they know."

"I would love that," I replied. Trevor smiled and leaned in close. He's not too big to be held—at least not yet.

"Dana, these are about who we were . . . but a little bit who we are," Susan said thoughtfully.

As we packed up the books, I was reassured that they still remembered. *The Pre-K East Life Book* had the effect they had intended years prior as 4- and 5-year-olds: to elicit memories and to tell the many stories that made up the history of our particular community of learners, the stories of us.

References

Adichie, C. (2009). *The danger of a single story.* Retrieved from www.ted.com/talks/chimamanda_adichie_the_danger_of_a_single_story.html

Anthropology. (n.d.). Retrieved from www.merriam-webster.com/dictionary/anthropology

Bahruth, R., & Steiner, S. (2000). Upstream in the mainstream: Pedagogy against the current. In S. Steiner, H. Krank, P. McLaren, & R. Bahruth (Eds.), *Freirean pedagogy, praxis, and possibilities: Projects for the new millennium* (pp. 120–147). New York, NY: Falmer Press.

Barnett, W. S. (1996). *Lives in the balance: Age-27 benefit-cost analysis of the High/Scope Perry preschool program.* Ypsilanti, MI: High/Scope Press.

Baumann, J. F., Jones, L. A., & Seifert-Kessell, N. (1993). Using think alouds to enhance children's comprehension monitoring abilities. *The Reading Teacher, 47*(3), 184–193.

Bentley, D. F. (2013). *Everyday artists: Inquiry and creativity in the early childhood classroom.* New York, NY: Teachers College Press.

Bentley, D. F., & Souto-Manning, M. (2018). "We were marching for our equal rights": Political literacies in the early childhood classroom. In N. Yelland & D. F. Bentley (Eds.), *Connecting reconceptualist thinking with early childhood education practices: Found in translation* (pp. 91–110). New York, NY: Routledge.

Berg, A., & Mensah, F. (2014). De-marginalizing science in the elementary classroom by coaching teachers to address perceived dilemmas. *Education Policy Analysis Archives, 22*(57), 1–32. doi: dx.doi.org/10.14507/epaa.v22n57.2014

Boal, A. (1979). *Theatre of the oppressed.* New York, NY: Urizen Books.

Boal, A. (1995). *The rainbow of desire: The Boal method of theatre and therapy.* New York, NY: Routledge.

Bodrova, E. (2008). Make-believe play versus academic skills: A Vygotskian approach to today's dilemma of early childhood education. *European Early Childhood Research Journal, 16*(3), 357–369.

Brady, I. (2009). Foreword. M. Pendergast, C. Leggo, & P. Sameshima (Eds.), *Poetic inquiry: Vibrant voices in social sciences* (pp. xi–xvi). Rotterdam, The Netherlands: Sense Publishers.

Brandt, D. (1998). Sponsors of literacy. *College Composition and Communication, 49*(2), 165–185.

Britton, J. (2003). Spectator role and the beginnings of writing. In V. Villanueva (Ed.), *Cross-talk in comp theory* (2nd ed., pp. 151–174). Urbana, IL: National Council of Teachers of English.

Cahnmann-Taylor, M., & Souto-Manning, M. (2010). *Teachers act up! Creating multicultural learning communities through theatre.* New York, NY: Teachers College Press.

Campbell, F. A., Breitmayer, B., & Ramey, C. T. (1986). Disadvantaged single teenage mothers and their children: Consequences of free educational day care. *Family Relations, 35*(1), 63–68.

Campbell, F. A., & Ramey, C. T. (1994). Effects of early intervention on intellectual and academic achievement: A follow-up study of children from low-income families. *Child Development, 65*(2), 684–689.

Campbell, F. A., & Ramey, C. T. (1995). Cognitive and school outcomes for high-risk African American students at middle adolescence: Positive effects of early intervention. *American Education Research Journal, 32*(4), 743–772.

Clarke, S. H., & Campbell, F. A. (1998). Can intervention early prevent crime later?: The Abecedarian project compared with other programs. *Early Childhood Research Quarterly, 13*(2), 319–343.

Clay, M. M. (2000). *Concepts about print: What have children learned about printed language?* Portsmouth, NH: Heinemann

Clay, M. M. (2013). *An observation survey of early literacy achievement* (3rd ed.). Portsmouth, NH: Heinemann.

Cooper, P., Capo, K., Mathes, B., & Gray, L. (2007). One authentic early literacy practice and three standardized tests: Can a storytelling curriculum measure up? *Journal of Early Childhood Teacher Education, 28*(3), 251–275.

Dewey, J. (1902). *The child and the curriculum.* Chicago, IL: University of Chicago Press.

Dewey, J. (1938). *Experience and education.* New York, NY: Macmillan.

Diamond, A. (2010). The evidence base for improving school outcomes by addressing the whole child and addressing skills and attitudes, not just content. *Early Education and Development, 21*(5), 780–793.

Dyson, A. H. (1990a). Symbol makers, symbol weavers: How children link play, pictures, and print. *Young Children, 45*(2), 50–57.

Dyson, A. H. (1990b). Weaving possibilities: Rethinking metaphors for early literacy development. *The Reading Teacher, 44*(3), 202–213.

Dyson, A. H. (1994a). Confronting the split between "the child" and children: Toward new curricular visions of the child writer. *English Education, 26*(1), 12–28.

Dyson, A. H. (1994b). I'm gonna express myself: The politics of story in children's worlds. In A. H. Dyson & C. Genishi (Eds.), *The need for story: Cultural diversity in classroom and community* (pp. 155–171). Urbana, IL: National Council of Teachers of English.

Dyson, A. H. (2008). On listening to child composers: Beyond "fix-its." In C. Genishi & A. Goodwin (Eds.), *Diversities in early childhood education: Rethinking and doing* (pp. 13–27). New York, NY: Routledge.

Dyson, A. H., & Genishi, C. (Eds.). (1994). *The need for story: Cultural diversity in classroom and community.* Urbana, IL: National Council of Teachers of English.

Edwards, C., Gandini, L., & Forman, G. (2011). *The hundred languages of children: The Reggio Emilia experience in transformation* (3rd ed.). Santa Barbara, CA: Praeger.

Emdin, C. (2016). *For White folks who teach in the hood . . . and the rest of y'all too: Reality pedagogy and urban education*. Boston, MA: Beacon Press.
Epstein, A. (2014). Social studies in preschool? Yes! *Young Children, 69*(1), 78–83.
Freire, P. (1970). *Pedagogy of the oppressed*. New York, NY: Continuum.
Freire, P. (1998). *Teachers as cultural workers: Letters to those who dare teach*. Boulder, CO: Westview Press.
Freire, P. (2000). *Pedagogy of the oppressed* (30th anniversary ed.). New York, NY: Bloomsbury.
Freire, P., & Macedo, D. (1987). *Literacy: Reading the word and the world*. Westport, CT: Bergin & Garvey.
Freire, P., & Macedo, D. (1995). A dialogue: Culture, language, and race. *Harvard Educational Review, 65*(3), 377–402.
Freppon, P., & Dahl, K. (1991). Learning about phonics in a whole language classroom. *Language Arts, 68*(3), 190–197.
Gartrell, D. (2012). *Education for a civil society: How guidance teaches young children democratic life skills*. Washington, DC: National Association for the Education of Young Children.
Genishi, C., & Dyson, A. H. (1984). *Language assessment in the early years*. Norwood, NJ: Ablex.
Genishi, C., & Dyson, A. H. (2009). *Children, language, and literacy: Diverse learners in diverse times*. New York, NY, & Washington, DC: Teachers College Press and National Association for the Education of Young Children.
Genishi, C., & Dyson, A.H. (2012). Racing to the top: Who's accounting for the children? *Bank Street Occasional Papers, 27*, 18–20.
Ginsburg, H., Lee, J., & Boyd, J. (2008). Mathematics education for young children: What it is and how to promote it. *Society for Research in Child Development's Social Policy Report, 22*(1), 1–23. Retrieved from files.eric.ed.gov/fulltext/ED521700.pdf
Graue, M. E. (1992). *Ready for what? Constructing meanings of readiness for kindergarten*. Albany, NY: State University of New York Press.
Graves, D. (1983). *Writing: Teachers & children at work*. Portsmouth, NH: Heinemann.
Graves, D. (1985). All children can write. *Learning Disabilities Focus, 1*(1), 36–43.
Greene, A., Ellis, V., & Simecek, K. (2016). Actual texts, possible meanings: The uses of poetry and the subjunctification of experience. *Changing English, 23*(4), 351–362.
Greene, M. (1973). *Teacher as stranger: Educational philosophy for the modern age*. Belmont, CA: Wadsworth Publishing.
Halbwachs, M. (1992). *On collective memory*. Chicago, IL: The University of Chicago Press.
Halliday, M.A.K. (1993). Towards a language-based theory of learning. *Linguistics and Education, 5*(2), 93–116.
Hart, B. & Risley, T.R. (2003). The early catastrophe: The 30 million word gap by age 3. *American Educator*, *27*(1), 4–9.
Hatch, J. A. (2002). Accountability shovedown: Resisting the standards movement in early childhood education. *Phi Delta Kappan, 83*(6), 457–462.
Heath, S. B. (1983). *Ways with words: Language, life and work in communities and classrooms*. Cambridge, England: Cambridge University Press.

Helm, J., & Katz, L. (2011). *Young investigators: The project approach in the early years* (2nd ed.). New York, NY: Teachers College Press.

International Literacy Association. (2018). *Why literacy?* Retrieved from www.literacyworldwide.org/about-us/why-literacy

Ladson-Billings, G. (1995). "But that's just good teaching!" The case for culturally relevant pedagogy. *Theory into Practice, 34*(3), 159–165.

Ladson-Billings, G. (2012). *Cultural competency.* Retrieved from www.youtube.com/watch?v=XSE8nxxZN5s

Lester, J. (2005). *Let's talk about race.* New York, NY: Amistad.

Licona, A. C., & Chávez, K. R. (2015). Relational literacies and their coalitional possibilities. *Peitho: Journal of the Coalition of Women Scholars in the History of Rhetoric & Composition, 18*(1), 96–107.

Licona, A. C., & Russell, S. T. (2013). Transdisciplinary and community literacies: Shifting discourses and practices through new paradigms of public scholarship and action-oriented research. *Community Literacy Journal, 8*(1), 1–7.

Lindfors, J. W. (2008). *Children's language: Connecting reading, writing, and talk.* New York, NY: Teachers College Press.

Lindfors, J. W., & Townsend, J. S. (1999). *Teaching language arts: Learning through dialogue.* Urbana, IL: National Council of Teachers of English.

Malaguzzi, L. (1998). History, ideas and basic philosophy: An interview with Lella Gandini. In C. Edwards, L. Gandini, & G. Forman (Eds.), *The hundred languages of children: The Reggio Emilia approach—advanced reflections* (pp. 27–45). Westport, CT: Ablex.

Marsh, J. (2005). *Popular culture, new media and digital literacy in early childhood.* Abingdon, England: Routledge.

Meier, D. (2004). *The young child's memory for words: Developing first and second language and literacy.* New York, NY: Teachers College Press.

Moll, L., Amanti, C., Neff, D., & Gonzalez, N. (1992). Funds of knowledge for teaching: Using a qualitative approach to connect homes and classrooms. *Theory into Practice, 31*(2), 132–141.

National Association for the Education of Young Children (NAEYC). (2009). *Developmentally appropriate practice in early childhood programs serving children from birth through age 8: A position statement of the National Association for the Education of Young Children.* Washington, DC: Author. Retrieved from www.naeyc.org/files/naeyc/file/positions/position%20statement%20Web.pdf

National Center on Universal Design for Learning. (2012). *What is UDL?* Retrieved from www.udlcenter.org/aboutudl/whatisudl

National Council for the Social Studies (NCSS). (2010). *National curriculum standards for the social studies: A framework for teaching, learning, and assessment.* Silver Spring, MD: NCSS. Retrieved from www.socialstudies.org/about

National Council for the Social Studies (NCSS). (2018). *About National Council for the Social Studies: What is social studies?* Silver Spring, MD: NCSS. Retrieved from www.socialstudies.org/about

National Research Council. (1996). *National science education standards.* Washington, DC: National Academy Press.

NGSS Lead States. (2013). *Next generation science standards: For states, by states.* Washington, DC: The National Academies Press.

Owocki, G., & Goodman, Y. M. (2002). *Kidwatching: Documenting children's literacy development*. Portsmouth, NH: Heinemann.

Paley, V. G. (1990). *The boy who would be a helicopter: The uses of storytelling in the classroom*. Cambridge, MA: Harvard University Press.

Paley, V. G. (2004). *A child's work: The importance of fantasy play*. Chicago, IL: The University of Chicago Press.

Paley, V. G. (2007). Goldilocks and her sister: An anecdotal guide to the doll corner. *Harvard Educational Review, 77*(2), 144–151.

Paley, V. G. (2014). *Boys and girls: Superheroes in the doll corner* (new ed.). Chicago, IL: The University of Chicago Press.

Ray, K. W., & Glover, M. (2008). *Already ready: Nurturing writers in preschool and kindergarten*. Portsmouth, NH: Heinemann.

Richardson, L. (2000). Writing: A method of inquiry. In N. Denzin & Y. Lincoln (Eds.), *Handbook of qualitative research* (2nd ed., pp. 923–948). Thousand Oaks, CA: SAGE.

Rinaldi, C. (2006). *In dialogue with Reggio Emilia: Listening, researching and learning*. Abingdon, England: Routledge.

Rosenblatt, L. (1978). *The reader, the text, the poem: The transactional theory of the literary work*. Carbondale, IL: Southern Illinois University Press.

Routman, R. (2003). *Reading essentials: The specifics you need to teach reading well*. Portsmouth, NH: Heinemann.

Rowe, D. W. (1994). *Preschoolers as authors: Literacy learning in the social world of the classroom*. Cresskill, NJ: Hampton Press.

Seefeldt, C., Castle, S., & Falconer, R. (2010). *Social studies for the preschool/primary child* (8th ed.). Boston, MA: Merrill.

Simecek, K., & Ellis, V. (2017). The uses of poetry: Renewing an educational understanding of a language art. *Journal of Aesthetic Education, 51*(1), 98–114.

Sloan, G. (2001). But is it poetry? *Children's Literature in Education, 32*(1), 45–56.

Smith, L. (1953). *The unreluctant years: A critical approach to children's literature*. Chicago, IL: American Library Association.

Soja, E. (1996). *Thirdspace: Journeys to Los Angeles and other real-and-imagined places*. Malden, MA: Blackwell.

Souto-Manning, M. (2010). *Freire, teaching, and learning: Culture circles across contexts*. New York, NY: Peter Lang.

Souto-Manning, M. (2013). *Multicultural teaching in the early childhood classroom: Approaches, strategies, and tools, preschool–2nd grade*. New York, NY: Teachers College Press.

Souto-Manning, M. (2019). Toward praxically just transformations: Interrupting racism in teacher education. *Journal of Education for Teaching, 45*(1), 97–113. Retrieved from doi.org/10.1080/02607476.2019.1550608

Souto-Manning, M., Lugo Llerena, C., Martell, J., Salas Maguire, A., & Arce-Boardman, A. (2018). *No more culturally irrelevant teaching*. Portsmouth, NH: Heinemann.

Souto-Manning, M., & Martell, J. (2016). *Reading, writing, and talk: Inclusive teaching strategies for diverse learners, K–2*. New York, NY: Teachers College Press.

Souto-Manning, M., & Yoon, H. S. (2018). *Reading and rewriting worlds: Rethinking early literacies*. London, England: Routledge.

Verba, S. (2006). Fairness, equality, and democracy: Three big words. *Social Research, 73*(2), 499–540.

Vygotsky, L. S. (1978). *Mind in society: The development of higher psychological processes.* Cambridge, MA: Harvard University Press.

Wells, G. (1994). The complementary contributions of Halliday and Vygotsky to a "language-based theory of learning." *Linguistics and Education, 6*(1), 41–90.

Wilhelm, J. D. (2001). *Improving comprehension with think-aloud strategies: Modeling what good readers do.* New York, NY: Scholastic.

Windschitl, M., Thompson, J., & Braaten, M. (2018). *Ambitious science teaching.* Cambridge, MA: Harvard Education Press.

Wohlwend, K. (2013). *Literacy playshop: New literacies, popular media, and play in the early childhood classroom.* New York, NY: Teachers College Press.

Yoon, J., & Onchwari, J. (2006). Teaching young children science: Three key points. *Early Childhood Education Journal, 33*(6), 419–423.

Index

The letter *f* after a page number refers to a figure.

About the Authors

The coauthors of this book, Dana Frantz Bentley and Mariana Souto-Manning, met in New York City in 2008 and have been collaborating and growing together ever since.

Dana Frantz Bentley is a classroom teacher in the prekindergarten program at Buckingham Browne and Nichols School in Cambridge, Massachusetts. She is also an assistant professor in the early childhood program at the Lesley University Graduate School of Education. Dana has been an early childhood teacher for over 17 years, working with young children from infancy to age 7 in diverse, urban settings in Boston and New York. In her teaching and writing, Dana focuses on social justice work with young children, studying children's emerging political literacies, as well as her own pedagogy as an antibias educator. Dana's writing has been featured in a wide range of early childhood journals, as well as in her books: *Everyday Artists* from Teachers College Press and her coedited volume *Found in Translation* from Routledge (with Nicola Yelland). Her dual role as a scholar/teacher allows her to question and investigate theory in practice in the ever-evolving realities of today's young children.

Mariana Souto-Manning is Professor of Early Childhood and Teacher Education in the Department of Curriculum and Teaching at Teachers College, Columbia University. She holds additional academic appointments at the University of Iceland and King's College London. Souto-Manning is founding co-director of the Center for Innovation in Teacher Education and Development (CITED). Her research examines inequities and injustices in early childhood teaching and teacher education, critically (re)centering methodologies and pedagogies on the lives, values, and experiences of intersectionally minoritized people of color. Mariana regularly collaborates with teachers. Throughout her career, Mariana has authored more than 100 articles and book chapters, as well as nine books, including the award-winning *Reading, Writing, and Talk: Inclusive Teaching Strategies for Diverse Learners, K–2* (with Jessica Martell). She is recipient of a number of research awards, including the 2011 American Educational Research Association (AERA) Division K Innovations in Research on Diversity in Teacher Education Award and the 2017 AERA Teaching and Teacher Education Mid-Career Award.